THE BEST PRICE FOR YOUR HOME IS THE LOVE PRICE

5 STEPS TO SELL YOUR HOME FOR MORE, SOONER!!

PETER HUTTON

Published in 2015 in Australia by Hutton & Hutton.

Email: peter@huttonandhutton.com.au

Website: www.huttonandhutton.com.au

Copyright © Hutton & Hutton 2015

This Book is not intended to provide personalised real estate sales and marketing advice. The author and the publisher specifically disclaim any liability, loss or risk which is incurred as a consequence, directly or indirectly, of the use and application of any of the contents of this work.

ALL RIGHTS RESERVED. This book contains material protected under International and Federal Copyright Laws and Treaties. Any unauthorised reprint or use of this material is prohibited. No part of this book may be reproduced or transmitted in any form or by any means, electronic or mechanical, including photocopying, recording, or by any information storage and retrieval system without express written permission from the author / publisher.

Typesetting and cover design by: Book Cover Café

ISBN:
978-0-646-93824-0 (pbk)
978-0-646-93825-7 (ebk)

For bulk orders of this book or general media enquiries, please contact the publisher on the above email address.

ACKNOWLEDGEMENTS

"Anytime you see a turtle up on top of a fence post, you know he had some help."
— ALEX HALEY

My completion of this book could not have been accomplished without the support of my talented and beautiful wife, Karen Hutton.

So to you Karen goes my deepest gratitude. This book would never have turned out as well as it has without your encouragement, guidance, feedback, input and editing genius. My heartfelt thanks. I love you.

To everyone else who gave me feedback on my manuscript (you know who you are) I thank you for your honesty, invaluable suggestions and positive encouragement. It's a better book for it.

PREFACE

Let me prepare you, the reader, for a "This is how I speak" style of writing. To all the wordsmiths, my English teachers at school, the writers of beautiful prose and poetry - I'm no Ernest Hemingway and I do not mean to disrespect you!

    I communicate best when I write how I speak. I hope you'll enjoy the conversational style and appreciate the intent to inform - as if it was just you and me, talking together, telling it how it is!

CONTENTS

INTRODUCTION
What's the love price and why should you care?   9

STEP 1: PLAN   17
  1: Beware the one size fits all plan   18
  2: Getting the love price starts with why   30
  3: Saving money vs. Making money plan   35
  4: Communication - acting in your best interest   39
  5: Prescribing the best plan for you   44

STEP 2: PRICE   53
  6: The 6 dynamics that influence the 'sold price' of your home   54
  7: How realistic is your price?   58
  8: The market trend is your friend   63
  9: Days on market - the lethal stigma   67
  10: The price deterrent   73
  11: Choosing the best method of sale   78
  12: Your agent just doesn't 'get' price variation strategies   87

STEP 3: PRESENT   95
  13: The wow factor!!   97

14: What agents don't tell you about decluttering and styling	101
15: The hero shot - capturing wow!!	107
16: The 7 deadly sins of open home presentation	110

STEP 4: PROMOTE	**116**
17: How property sellers pay dearly for so-called 'free' advertising	118
18: Falling for those 'large database of buyers' claims	122
19: Getting on your home buyer's radar	125
20: How to get better results from your online advertising	131
21: Turning your internet ad into click bait	137
22: How to describe your home so buyers come running	142
23: Your home selling promotion checklist	146

STEP 5: PITCH	**151**
24: Getting buyers to make a buying decision, sooner!!	153
25: The open home sales pitch - do's & don'ts	158
26: After the open home - buyer follow-up	164
27: Why an early offer could be your best offer	169
28: Negotiating 'the love price' for your home	171
29: Auction day - giving back control to you	178
30: When your buyer has the upper hand	185

A FINAL WORD	**187**
AGENT QUESTIONNAIRE	**190**
ABOUT PETER HUTTON	**199**

INTRODUCTION
WHAT'S THE LOVE PRICE AND WHY SHOULD YOU CARE?

Bill (not his real name), a past client, called me one Saturday. "Hey Pete, did you see that villa being advertised for 'offers over $1,000,000' by XYZ Agency (another made up name) in today's property section of the Courier Mail?" Bill excitedly asked.

"Yeah I did Bill. I know that property. It would be p-e-r-f-e-c-t for you and your family mate," I replied.

"That's what we think. We want to buy it. Only thing is, we don't want to have to deal with XYZ, we were hoping we could buy it through you," Bill asked nervously.

"Bill I'd love to help you. But not sure if the listing agent will be open to that. Let me see what I can do," I said.

A few calls later, I managed to set up a 'conjunctional' arrangement where the listing agent allowed me to deal directly with his seller. An unusual arrangement, but welcomed by Bill and myself.

With great optimism, I presented Bill's cash offer of $1,025,000 in writing to the seller.

But here's the thing. Sometimes in real estate what appears to be well-founded optimism is actually unfounded and the prelude to frustration. Here's what happened...

Picture this. Enthusiastically, I present my buyer's offer to the seller. An offer that's not only $25,000 over the advertised asking price but is cold hard cash with no extra conditions; and the seller's response? Get this, he says, "Sorry Peter, but that's not what we're after. Your buyer's way off."

"Really? Way off? Is he just playing with me?" I thought.

I quickly replayed what he said in my mind and yep there it was, I think he said it with just a touch of laughter in his voice. He's just playing with me. PHEW.

So I waited a moment thinking he'd come clean and congratulate me on a job well done. Seconds went by. Buuuuuut...

Nope. No congratulations. Just silence. Maybe he's not joking I thought. Damn!!

Surprised by this unexpected dismissal of what I assumed was a lay down misere offer, I gathered myself and responded with, "I thought the ad said offers over $1,000,000. It is $25k over your asking price. So, ummmm, what were you expecting to get?"

With that, the seller's tone changed. The laughter in his voice left. His response was swift, unemotional and to the point... "We want $1.45 million. Peter, we're just not going to sell it for less than that."

No wonder the listing agent was so accommodating, so willing and happy for me to deal directly with his seller. I should have twigged to that.

So here we were, nearly a half a million dollars apart. That's a ridiculously BIG gap to close I thought.

Of course, Bill was gob smacked when I gave him the news. Of course he got angry. Of course he accused the listing agent of false and misleading advertising. Of course he threatened to call the Office of Fair Trading, the

INTRODUCTION

ACCC, the REIQ, ACA and Today Tonight. You name it, he was threatening to call them. He was a buyer scorned.

Anger and frustration can make a buyer walk away from a property. But despite Bill's anger and frustration threatening to derail the negotiations, something else kept him at the negotiation table.

Over the years I've found that even when a buyer is angry and frustrated, there can be another emotion, maybe under the surface of all the anger, that's really motivating their actions. I call that their 'core motivation'.

At the end of the day, it's all about a buyer's core motivation. If you understand that about your buyer, then getting to 'yes' in the negotiation happens sooner.

Bill expressed his core motivations loud and clear to me. Not directly as you may be thinking, but indirectly. I could hear it in his voice. I could see it in his body language. I could sense it in his actions.

Twenty years in real estate teaches you a thing or two about buyer motivation. From my experience, Bill clearly was being motivated by something other than the usual emotions agents talk about, like greed and the fear of loss.

What was motivating Bill would trump anger, frustration, greed and even fear. It's an emotion that can really drive a buyer towards what they want. It's an emotion that can move a buyer past insurmountable obstacles such as price. It's an emotion that can help a buyer go over their budget in pursuit of their dream home.

Yes, we were far apart in price, but that emotion, that core motivation that I could see in Bill, was telling me the gap could be closed.

Time and time again over the years, I witnessed the same powerful emotion that had brought Bill to the negotiation table, keep a buyer at the negotiation table, pause rational thinking and move a buyer rapidly towards making a 'buying decision'.

What was this powerful emotion that was driving Bill?

It was the EMOTIVE POWER of LOVE!! It happens when your buyer's actions become directed more so by their heart instead of their head.

How did the power of love play out for Bill and the seller?

It took five days of negotiation. Five days where Bill increased his offer in excruciatingly small increments of $25,000 a time. Some days he increased his offer multiple times. Five days where each and every incremental increase was rejected by the resolutely stubborn seller. Five days of holding my buyer's hand through his anger and frustration in trying to buy this property.

I remember my wife, Karen, asking me how the negotiations were progressing. I told her about how the buyer would threaten to walk after every new bid he made was rejected by the seller. I told her the seller was threatening to withdraw the property from sale if the buyer didn't come up to what they wanted. I told her I felt good about the negotiations despite the threats because as far as I was concerned, all signs (i.e. my buyer's core motivation) pointed to a sale.

When negotiating a sale like this, well any sale in fact, the agent needs to be acutely aware of the fiduciary nature of the relationship with their client (the seller of the property). The relationship between seller and agent places an agent in a position of trust, confidence and responsibility in which their foremost duty is to act in the best interests of their client and deal ethically with all parties involved in the property transaction.

That being said, it's a bit of a juggling act because you want to help both sides get what they want. That's tricky when the gap is so big. But it's very doable if you know how.

Oh, and it's only doable in the absence of manipulation. I believe agents who resort to manipulating buyers and/or sellers to get a sale, harm the natural, positive course a negotiation could have taken. Manipulation often results in the 'underselling' (in terms of price) of a property.

What was happening here was free of manipulation. It was a natural process. One that allowed the buyer's core motivation to dictate each of his 'next steps' in the negotiation. In the end...

...a SALE!!

The final price? A whopping $1,425,000!!!

The seller was over the moon. What was just as lovely though was how Bill was feeling. He too was over the moon. In the end, despite where the negotiations had started, it was a win-win for both parties.

Recently I bumped into Bill at the supermarket. "How's the villa?" I asked. "We couldn't be happier Pete. We love it there." Bill made no mention of the slow, drawn out negotiations and the price he ended up paying.

The moral of my story?

Plain and simple, there's a thing I call 'The LOVE Price'. When you trigger an emotional, 'HOT-BUTTON' response in your buyers, and fan the flames of love, you'll maximise the price your home will sell for. After your home is sold, some may even come to say that the price you achieved was no less than a 'record price', or they'll describe it as a 'premium price'. In any case, it'll be a price that often defies rational thinking.

FOR THE BUYER: 'The LOVE Price' is the price at which their love for the property motivates them to spend beyond a 'rational price' in order to secure the ownership of the property. In other words, they just have to have it.

FOR THE SELLER: 'The LOVE Price' is the point where their desire and usage for the money they'll get from the sale outweighs their desire and usage of retaining ownership over the property.

This book's primary focus is on how to get the buyer's love price to match or better the seller's love price and is dedicated to helping you, the home seller, tap into the 'emotive-power' of love to achieve 'The LOVE Price' for your home.

Over the years, I've developed a '5 Step Methodology' that when followed correctly ensures 'The LOVE Price' is paid.

They are...

STEP 1 – PLAN
STEP 2 – PRICE
STEP 3 – PRESENT
STEP 4 – PROMOTE
STEP 5 – PITCH

Following these 5 steps (from now on I'll be referring to them as the 5Ps) will not only fast-track your sale, it will ensure that you attract the right buyer/s for your home who will fall in love with it and will be prepared to pay 'The LOVE Price' to get it.

The fact is, 'The LOVE Price' and the 5Ps work spectacularly well. I've developed the 5P methodology over 20 years in real estate during which time I've sold close to 1,000 homes, been recognised internationally as "Australia's Best Estate Agent" and delivered keynote speeches on this subject throughout Australia.

It's my hope then, that this little book will save the reader, you, from the disappointment of not getting your home sold. Save you from wasting your time and money and most importantly, save you from underselling your home and missing out on getting 'The LOVE Price'.

In addition to showing you how to get 'The LOVE Price', this little book will answer sellers' most commonly asked questions before deciding which agent to list their home with.

They are...
- How will you get me the price I want for my property?
- What's the best method of sale?
- What's my property really worth?
- What do I need to do to my property so it sells for top dollar?
- How are you going to attract buyers to my property?
- What price, if any, should we advertise it at?
- How experienced are you at negotiating?

HOW TO GET MAXIMUM VALUE FROM THIS BOOK

I need to be straight with you.

In this book, I divulge my entire 5P methodology to getting 'The LOVE Price' that I've used to help many hundreds of sellers over the years.

However, I believe that making wild claims that everyone will succeed at getting 'The LOVE Price' for their home is stupid, and frankly, irresponsible.

You're welcome to share this book with your real estate agent. Oh sure, some of them will refuse to read it. They probably think they know better. But those that do read it, who are open to learn something new, will benefit from it and that's good for you, right?

I'm aware that many agents will accuse me of giving away too much information in this book. They'll fear that home sellers who read this book may no longer feel the need to employ an agent to sell their home. Maybe so. I don't concern myself about that. I believe in transparency, and I believe in empowering people by giving them knowledge.

This book is designed to empower home owners wanting top dollar for their property and who are willing to do what's necessary to get it. If that's you, great. I have a lot to give you. In this book, I'll map out exactly how I've achieved 'The LOVE Price' for countless home owners, and I'll show you how to do the same for your home.

The best way to receive maximum value from this book and the 5Ps is to read each section in order. Don't skip ahead. The five steps are designed specifically to build on each other. Great information is useless if we don't use it. So use it. From here on it's up to you.

STEP 1: **PLAN**

Recently a home seller asked me why they needed a plan if their agent was the one handling the sale of their home.

It sounded to me as if they were thinking of their home selling plan in simplistic terms. You know, a plan that really only addressed things like when the auction would be, dates and times for the open homes, scheduling of photography and placement of advertising, that sort of thing. Of course their agent would take care of all of that.

They probably also thought the agent would address things like how much they would get for their property and what it was going to cost them. Yeah sure, they're things an agent will certainly discuss with a seller too. But on top of all of that, there are some other crucial things sellers should plan for.

A home selling plan is much more than a timeline of actions the agent will take on your behalf: it's a tool for understanding how your home will achieve 'The LOVE Price'.

A proper home selling plan will help you monitor progress, hold yourself accountable, hold your agent accountable and control the fate of the sale. Of course, it'll help you choose the best agent for you to list with.

In this section of the book, I help you get clear on what the best plan is for you.

CHAPTER 1
BEWARE THE ONE SIZE FITS ALL PLAN

My apologies for the rant I'm about to go on in this chapter. Seems like it's the elephant in the room and no agent is prepared to say it, well at least publicly that is. What I'm about to expose will be a little controversial and I'm thinking a good number of agents reading this won't like it, but it has to be said...

There's a certain kind of home selling plan that mainstream agents follow that's not designed to get you 'The LOVE Price'.

Let me explain...

The LOVE Price doesn't just happen. It takes a plan. Well two actually. Your plan and your agent's plan.

So as much as you need a plan for how you want your sale to go, the agent needs a plan too. Buuuut...

Like the TV commercial "Oils ain't oils", similarly agent's plans ain't agent's plans.

What I mean is...

There are two distinct types of agent plans for selling residential real estate.

CHAPTER 1

The first and most common approach agents offer is pretty much a 'one-size-fits-all' plan to sell your home. (Beware this kind.)

The second type offered by a minority of agents is a 'tailor-made' custom plan, an individually designed, customised plan so to speak.

The problem is, it's hard for sellers to not only recognise the difference, but be in a position to determine which is better for them.

So let's start by getting to know what the generic, one-size-fits-all real estate plan looks like. It'll go something like this...

The agent will tell you they'll start with photographing your home. Maybe even get a video made. They'll recommend a floor plan or use a copy of what you have. Then they'll write the copy. They'll follow that by uploading it to their website, realestate.com.au and/or domain.com.au (if you're in Australia) and some other real estate online portals. They'll erect a signboard. They'll probably contact everyone in the street and let them know you're selling. They'll email their buyer database. If they have a magazine, they'll advertise the property in that. They'll show you options for advertising in the newspaper. They'll conduct open for inspections. They'll call buyers back after every inspection. They'll give you feedback after every inspection. If it's an auction, they'll set a date that's in roughly four weeks' time. They'll call you nearly every day with an update on their activities. They'll meet with you face-to-face at least once a week to discuss how the sale is progressing and voila there's your plan.

By the way, I regard all of those things as bare minimum activity in any home selling plan.

Of course there will be variations to the plan from agent to agent.

The method of sale will vary. Some agents will say it has to be auctioned. Others will argue auctions are bad and private treaty is better. Some agents will say all you need to do is advertise it on realestate.com.au because they say that's where all the buyers are. Others will swear by print media. Some will even say advertising of any form is a waste of time, and it's better to market it directly to a database of buyers.

(No wonder sellers find it confusing. Don't worry, this book will help you make sense of those differences so you can make an informed decision.)

There's nothing wrong with this kind of plan. As I said, it's common, and that's because agents do get results from a plan like this.

Here's the thing. You're reading this book because it's not about a result, it's about you getting the best result, 'The LOVE Price' for your home, right? Sure. That's what you want. Who wouldn't?!

But the BIG problem is, these 'one-size-fits-all' type plans to sell your home were never designed to get the best result for you or 'The LOVE Price'. They were designed just to get a sale.

To understand that, we first need to understand why so many agencies have gone the way of 'one-size-fits-all' instead of the customised, made-to-measure path.

A Brief History of 'One-Size-Fits-All'

The small business world was broadly introduced to the growth benefits that come with a 'one-size-fits-all' plan in 1995 when the book "The E-Myth Revisited" by Michael E. Gerber became a best seller. It was all about business growth through 'process'.

The burgeoning real estate agency groups at the time, especially those with big growth ambitions, seem to have taken notice of what Gerber was saying. Maybe that was just a coincidence, in any case, Gerber's book explains why businesses were so eager to adopt the 'one-size-fits-all' plan.

Gerber called it "the franchise phenomenon." He points out it all started in 1952 when Ray Kroc visited the McDonald brother's burger stand. Kroc was so taken with their business that he convinced the brothers to let him franchise their method and McDonald's was born.

CHAPTER 1

Here's what Gerber said about Kroc's interest in the McDonald's brother burger stand, "It worked like a Swiss watch! Hamburgers were produced in a way he'd never seen before - quickly, efficiently, inexpensively, and identically. Best of all, anyone could do it. He watched high school kids working with precision under the supervision of the owners, happily responding to the long lines of customers queued up in front of the stand. It became apparent to Ray Kroc that what the McDonald brothers had created was not just another hamburger stand but a money machine!"

What Ray Kroc discovered was a replicable business process and with it, he could guarantee customers would get the same burger and experience from each and every McDonald's store around the world. It's been the formula for McDonald's stellar growth.

Herein lies the obvious parallel with McDonald's growth and that of the large real estate franchise groups. By establishing a production-line, replicable, 'one-size-fits-all' type process, an agency could ensure a greater consistency amongst their sales people that would allow them to employ more and more sales agents and open more real estate offices. From there the agency and agency groups would grow and grow rapidly they did.

That's why agencies seeking growth tend to follow in McDonald's footsteps. It's the 'McDonaldised' approach to growing a real estate business.

McDonald's works because it is designed to serve the same thing to the masses whether they are rich, poor, skinny, or fat and whether they are buying breakfast, lunch or dinner.

That's pretty cool if you're selling burgers. But selling a home is not like selling a burger. Every home is different. Every seller is different. Every buyer is different. The market is dynamic. Each area is different and there's actually no 'one right way' to selling a home.

So although process provides consistency, and I'm all for that, the BIG problem with a 'one-size-fits-all' process is that it tries to standardise every home and home seller. It was never designed for the individual. It was designed primarily to facilitate business growth. It's a mass-produced solution and we all know a mass-produced service doesn't generally equate to the BEST quality service.

Here's an example of how this relates to selling real estate...

Big 'McDonaldised' agencies encourage their agents to list lots of properties. As many as possible. It's a numbers game for them. It's about dominating their market place. The 'one-size-fits-all' plan/process helps them do that. It's about mass-production and it's about turnover. All of which assists with their growth.

The problem is, a focus on turnover and trying to service lots of selling clients spreads the agent thin.

What I mean is, the more listings an agent has, the less time the agent has to work hands-on with their sellers and their homes on a one-to-one basis. That forces the busiest agents in a 'McDonaldised' agency to use other less experienced agents to take care of critical aspects of the sales process, such as buyer enquiry.

Another symptom of 'one-size-fits-all' often results in agents not being able to attend the open homes of their own listings. Instead, they get their less experienced personal assistant or rookie sales associate to handle property inspections with buyers.

It seems the bigger the agency, the less likely it is that the person you list your home with will be the one actually servicing all the buyer enquiry on your home.

Some of the busiest 'McAgents' (that's an agent who adheres to a 'McDonaldised' 'one-size-fits-all' process), can have as many as three or four personal assistants doing a lot of the work. Which often means their personal assistants handle buyer enquiry.

Is it just me? Wouldn't you think if you listed your home with an experienced agent, that you probably chose them because of their experience in the first place, that you'd get them actually handling all of the buyer enquiry?

Imagine if you needed heart surgery. You see a top heart surgeon and when it comes to the operation, it's the surgeon's trainee who operates. That's crazy. So is a rookie agent looking after crucial things like open homes and 'buyer call backs'.

I PUT IT TO YOU, 'ONE-SIZE-FITS-ALL' BENEFITS AN AGENCY'S GROWTH MORE THAN IT DOES THEIR SELLING CLIENTS

It's designed for transactions before anything else. It's designed for sales turnover. It's designed for mass appeal and frankly speaking, it also seems the masses are quite ok with selling through this kind of burger factory approach. This maybe because they don't know better, but probably because the established 'McAgents' are the ones they're most familiar with and familiarity equals security in the minds of most consumers. (Reality check: just because you're familiar with a brand doesn't mean they're the best now does it?)

Custom Service Vs. McAgent Service

Your franchise 'McAgent' will be following a fixed, one-size-fits-all process and that process is often dictated by 'head-office'. But is it the best fit for you, the home seller? Is it the best fit for your property? Is it the best fit for your local market? And finally, how does 'head-office' even know what's best for you and your property? Fact is, they don't.

Let's be absolutely clear about this, if you want 'The LOVE Price', regardless of who you list with, the agent must tailor make your home selling plan to best fit YOU.

Here in lies the hidden trap with choosing a franchise 'McAgency' as opposed to an independent, 'boutique' agency to list with. An independent agent isn't being dictated to by a 'head-office'. They are by definition, 'independent'. That's why they are more likely to offer you a custom, 'best fit' home selling solution.

A custom service also means you'll get a great deal more love, care and hands-on-attention to the fine details from an experienced, top agent. I believe it is THE first thing you'll need to plan for. To get 'The LOVE Price' you'll need a custom, 'best-fit' plan, not just any plan.

'THE LOVE PRICE' CAN'T BE ACHIEVED IF PROCESS IS PUT BEFORE INDIVIDUAL ATTENTION

'The LOVE Price' is the result of a customised, individualised plan, it is a plan that's custom built for the individual seller. That recognises the individual nature of the property and the individual needs of the BEST buyer/s for the property.

If you're thinking that sounds expensive, don't. A customised 'tailor-made' plan will cost you no more than a 'one-size-fits-all' plan. It could even save you money.

Deb and Brian's luxury, architectural home in Bardon was not only literally the best house in the street, it was one of, if not the best house in the area. On top of that, its uncommon, split-level design wasn't terribly young-family friendly, further narrowing the market in this predominantly young-family area.

The sellers hoped to sell for as close to $3,000,000 as possible. Only thing was, the comparative market appraisal estimated a realistic, likely price to be somewhere in the vicinity of $2,200,000 to $2,400,000. However, I should say there were sales in other more expensive areas where similar homes were selling for in the high two millions at the time. It was these out-of-area comparison properties we were leaning towards as an indicator of what was possible. There was one other outcome they desired and that was they hoped the buyer would lease back the property to them for twelve months. You'd be right in thinking what they hoped for was a tall order.

At the time, sellers of $3,000,000 properties were often being recommended by the 'McAgents' a marketing budget that equated to about 1% of the property's value. That would mean Brian and Deb were up for a $30,000 marketing spend. The 'McAgents' were also reticent to place a figure on the property, saying the market would decide (translation, they thought the sellers were over ambitious in terms of price). There was also a feeling the sellers got that they were suggesting the buyer would be local.

Taking a customised approach, I designed a plan that included a small degree of styling to improve the presentation in some key spaces and a marketing spend of less than $15,000. Also, instead of allocating the vast majority of the marketing budget to print advertisements, a proportion of the ad spend was allocated to engaging a publicist who wrote a 'personal interest piece' as a press release. All promotion was designed to appeal to who we believed was the ideal buyer. By the way, I disagreed with the 'McAgents' view of where the buyer would come from. I felt the buyer would be 'property specific' in their search criteria rather than the mainstream view they'd be local buyers. So my plan took into consideration that the buyer was an out-of-area buyer. We also targeted a buyer who'd be attracted to a lease back. The press release created over $100,000 worth of free publicity in several local and national newspaper publications (source: the publicist's analysis of the free press we received).

The result? We attracted the ideal buyer for the property who not only loved it but needed the twelve month lease back to make the deal work for them. Oh, and the final sold price? A record breaking $2,810,000.

This customised approach worked because it took into consideration the individual needs of the seller and the buyer, and reflected the unique nature of the property.

'The LOVE Price' happens when your agent stands for quality over quantity. It happens when your agent is hands on, rather than delegating to someone less experienced. It happens when your agent is more about love, care and attention to detail than putting sellers through a sausage machine 'process'.

How to spot a one-size-fits-all plan:

There are two indicators that the agent you're interviewing for the job of selling your home is a one-size-fits-all 'McAgent'.
1. The agent will try and convince you their preferred method of sale is the all-round, best method of sale to sell property. So instead of providing you the various options and unbiasedly explaining the pros and cons of each method, they'll simply just tell you 'private treaty' is better than 'auction' and vice versa. Alternatively, they'll explain the pros and cons for each but pitch it to you in such a way that ensures you choose the option they're biased towards.
2. When it comes to advertising your property, they'll present you with an off-the-shelf advertising plan. Often the 'McAgent' will offer you three cleverly bundled up off-the-shelf, advertising packages for you to choose from. Typically the packages will be named something like, 'Bronze', 'Silver' and 'Gold'. The idea is by giving you three options of various expense from cheap to expensive, your guard will come

CHAPTER 1

down and predictably as most sellers do, you'll choose the middle cost option. Of course that's what the 'McAgent' was hoping (expecting) you'd do.

Comparing 'One-size-fits-all' to a 'Customised' service - a snapshot

2 TYPES OF REAL ESTATE SERVICE

'ONE-SIZE-FITS-ALL' SERVICE:
- is about high volume not quality
- not personalised to you or your property - it's a mass-produced service to fit any property
- claims to save you money
- 'head-office' can dictate HOW they market your property
- generally NOT a high quality service
- is about finding any buyer, but possibly NOT the best buyer for your property

'CUSTOMISED' SERVICE:
- is about quality not high volume
- perfectly matches your needs, wants, desires and concerns
- 'best-fit' property selling solution for you
- perfectly matches your property, to your *BEST* buyer who'll value your property the most
- a tailor-made plan designed to make you money and get you 'The LOVE Price'

The moral of this chapter?

'One-size-fits-all' may get your property sold, but it's NOT really designed to get you 'The LOVE Price'.

To be fair though, I should point out not all agents working within a 'McAgency' group stick strictly to a 'McDonaldised', one-size-fits-all process. They are however the exception to the rule.

It's also fair to say that sellers tend to place their trust in the agent they list with more so than the real estate agency itself. So provided the agent you list with isn't your typical 'McAgent', and provided they understand how 'The LOVE Price' is created, you'll be in good hands.

Also, please don't think that I'm saying all 'multiple office agency groups' are 'McDonaldised' agencies. I'm not. There are some great agency groups that don't fall into the 'McDonaldised' model. These groups don't resemble your typical big franchise, copy-and-paste, chain. They tend to be the smaller groups, often a boutique independent brand that has partner offices in several locations and who offer more of a customised service.

'The LOVE Price' doesn't just happen... it's the result of customised planning, customised service, customised execution, customised care and customised attention to detail.

The rest of this section of the book will cover all aspects of planning. With the right customised plan you can get 'The LOVE Price' for your home.

3 Hot Tips To Get 'The LOVE Price':

1. 'One-size-fits-all' is more about facilitating growth of an agency than facilitating the seller getting 'The LOVE Price'.
2. Many of the BIG agency groups are driven by growth. To get the growth they want, they have to 'McDonaldise' their processes to some extent. Some more than others. That's got nothing to do with getting 'The LOVE Price'.
3. 'The LOVE Price' happens when the home selling plan takes into consideration the individual needs of the seller and the buyer, and reflects the unique nature of the property and the property market at the time of going onto the market. It's all about 'best fit'.

CHAPTER 2
GETTING THE LOVE PRICE STARTS WITH WHY

So now that we know 'The LOVE Price' is the result of a tailor-made, customised plan as opposed to a 'McDonaldised' process, you can start developing your personalised 'home selling plan' around what you want from the sale. This includes working out who's the best agent for you.

The first place to start developing your home selling plan to get 'The LOVE Price' is 'why'. That is, you have to ask yourself, "Why am I *REALLY* selling?"

It may be a pretty obvious place to start, but you'll be surprised how often home sellers list with an agent and aren't absolutely 100% clear why they're selling. Sounds crazy doesn't it? But there's a lot more to answering this question of 'why' than you may be thinking right now.

The BIG reason you need great clarity about why you're selling is because it'll dramatically improve your chances of getting 'The LOVE Price'. I call it your 'BIG Why' for that very reason.

It's all about your level of commitment to the sale. This is key. Let me explain...

CHAPTER 2

It takes commitment for your home selling plan to play out as you hope. You'll have to be 100% committed to the sale and you'll want your agent to be 100% committed too, right?

What I've found is, the agent's degree of commitment to your sale will be proportional to your own commitment to it.

For you to be 100% committed to selling will require you to be absolutely clear on your 'BIG Why'.

There is no such thing as the right 'BIG Why'. Whatever it is will work, provided it connects you on an emotional level that motivates you.

I've found 'love' to be THE greatest emotional motivator. Sellers who are motivated by 'love' tend to do what it takes to get 'The LOVE Price'. When you clearly establish what you'd love from the sale, and provided that next step excites you, you'll no doubt be motivated to do what it takes to get 'The LOVE Price'.

Friends of mine, Paul and Sally (made up names for privacy purposes), were selling their beach holiday home and they'd engaged a local agent to handle the sale. But the sale wasn't going well at all. Six months on, they still hadn't sold.

Sally approached me for advice. She wanted some ideas on what they could be doing differently to get it sold. Apparently the agent was confident the price was right. Sally and Paul felt the same way. What was concerning them was other properties in the same location were selling a lot faster. Sally was really confused and frustrated by this.

Before I could help with ideas, I needed to understand why they wanted to sell. So I asked Sally. Here's what she said...

"I'm the one that wants it sold the most. I'm not sure if Paul is as committed to the sale. We just don't use it much these days. It's a waste. So I think we should sell it."

I then asked Sally what were their plans with the money they got from the sale.

Sally explained, "We're not 100% clear on that. So nothing concrete at this stage. I think I know what I want to do with it. But Paul can't make his mind up. So I haven't forced the issue with him. I thought we'd wait till after it had sold to decide."

When I heard this, alarm bells started ringing. I could see that Sally and Paul's lack of shared commitment in the sale was acting as a roadblock to the sale. They had no 'BIG Why'. I needed them to get thinking about their 'BIG Why'.

"So Sally, what would you love to do with the money?" I asked.

"Well if it was just up to me I'd love to buy a run-down house somewhere close to home. Something we could renovate. We've done little projects like that years ago when we just got married. It was fun working on it together. I'd love to do that again," Sally said smiling.

"And Paul, would he like to do that?" I asked.

"I think he would. He probably thinks though that he'll have to do all the hard work like he did back then. Paul is so busy at work, he probably thinks he doesn't have the time."

"So what if you worked out a way that Paul didn't have to do all the hard work, would he go for that?"

Sally replied to my question enthusiastically, "I think he would. He has that property developer mind. You know, loves to add value to property for a profit. That excites him."

"So Sally maybe sit down with Paul and discuss it with him. Sounds like he'd love to do a project provided he didn't have to do all the hard work. If it turns out that's what he'd love to do, won't that mean you two will be 100% committed to the sale of your holiday home so you can start your project?" I suggested.

Sally took my advice and had that conversation with Paul. Paul loved the idea. Now they both had a shared plan for the sale. They had found their 'BIG Why' and that meant they were now both 100% committed to the sale.

CHAPTER 2

A couple of weeks later Sally called me to let me know that they had a contract on the property for a price marginally below their asking price.

It turns out prior to Sally and Paul getting clear on their plan, the agent that was selling for them was thinking they'd never sell. He'd formed that impression through speaking with Paul on several occasions. In those conversations with their agent, Paul used language like "We're not in a hurry to sell" and "If we don't get our full asking price we won't be selling" and "We don't need to sell." Paul was sometimes quite unresponsive to their agent's attempts to contact him. No wonder their agent found it hard to sell it. Paul's obvious non-commitment to the sale rubbed off on their agent.

That all changed when Paul and Sally spoke to their agent after locking in their new plan. Their agent could obviously see they were now 100% committed. That gave him hope. What that meant was, instead of thinking his sellers weren't motivated to sell and there was little point in presenting them an offer below their asking price (in the past Paul had said if they didn't get their asking price they wouldn't sell), the agent pulled out all the stops to get buyers through the property to get it sold. Two weeks later it was sold.

Please don't underestimate what I'm saying here. It may sound a little esoteric, but your agent's attitude is EVERYTHING when it comes to getting you 'The LOVE Price'.

When you know your 'BIG Why', it's amazing the results that can be created. It can happen fast too, just like it did for Sally and Paul. Your plan then must address your 'BIG Why'. It forms the foundation stone of your plan.

2 Hot Tips To Get 'The LOVE Price':

1. To get 'The LOVE Price' you have to be 100% committed to the sale. If you're not fully committed to the sale, how can you expect your agent to be fully committed?
2. Commitment comes from knowing your 'BIG Why'. That's the core emotional motivator behind your decision to sell. So what's your 'BIG Why' for selling your home? When you can answer that, you'll have taken the first step in getting 'The LOVE Price' for your home.

CHAPTER 3
SAVING MONEY VS. MAKING MONEY PLAN

When you boil your home selling plan down, it's either going to be about saving you money or making you money.

Those sellers trying to SAVE MONEY hit the phones and/or the internet to conduct a quasi-interview with as many agents as possible, in an attempt to shortlist 2 or 3 potential agencies.

The aim of this process is simple - to see which of the agencies are flexible on their fees and how much they charge for advertising.

Then, they'll only interview those agents that agree to discount, without taking into consideration the differences between their services. More importantly, no consideration is made to the differences between what that agent will do for your bottom line.

When you really think about it, choosing an agent is all about the bottom line. It's about what's left over after paying fees and marketing expenses.

So there's a much smarter strategy of ensuring you save money.

It's simple really. You make your home selling plan about the 'gross' sold price you achieve and that will positively affect your 'net return'.

Focusing more on trying to save money will only cause you to cut corners in the presentation of your home; cut corners in your marketing; and cut corners in how your agent handles the negotiations. When you cut corners like that, your agent will be under-selling your home.

'Cut-price' agents and 'flat-rate-commission' agents aren't known for high sale prices. They're known for cutting corners and doing it on the cheap. All they're offering are cheap fees. A cheap agent is more likely to equate to a cheap sold price for your home which means less money for you.

Here's what to do. Start by interviewing 3 different agents. You'll treat this a little bit like you're interviewing a new employee. Yes, that's right, shop around, but not on price. You see, shopping purely on price could ironically be the costliest decision you make. Shop around on agent expertise, sales strategy and commitment; that's the answer.

So here's the thing, you need to ask the agents you're interviewing (to list your home with) some key questions that will reveal how they plan to achieve 'The LOVE Price' for your home before proceeding any further.

ASK THEM:

- "How will you promote my property and how will you get me the highest price? What's your strategy? Give me some case studies that prove to me your process/strategy is about netting me more $$$."
- "What value-adding services do you offer and how do these services filter through to my bottom line?"
- "Do you offer a Service Pledge or Guarantee? What's your undertaking if I need to enact them?"
- "Tell me about your experience and success selling similar properties to mine."
- "I'd like the names and phone numbers of several vendors you've sold for."
- "Can you show me some testimonials that demonstrate specifically how you've helped your clients?"

CHAPTER 3

To help you select the best real estate agent for the incredibly important and complicated job of selling your property, at the end of the book you'll find a questionnaire that you can use to interview them. It's titled "21 QUESTIONS TO UNCOVER THE AGENT BEST SUITED TO GETTING YOU 'THE LOVE PRICE' FOR YOUR HOME". You'll also find a link to PDF of the questionnaire which you can print off.

'Saving money' vs 'making money' - a snapshot

'SAVE MONEY' VS 'MAKE MONEY'

SELLERS WITH A **'SAVE MONEY'** PLAN:
- their focus is predominantly on how much money they can save
- often enticed by discounted commission
- often enticed by free advertising
- list with an agent based on how much they can save and NOT on how much money they can make

SELLERS WITH A **'MAKE MONEY'** PLAN:
- aim is to sell their property for a premium price
- focus is on how much money they can make; that is, how much they net from the sale
- list with an agent who can introduce the highest number of buyers to their property
- list with an agent who is skilled at marketing, sales and negotiation
- invests in a cost-effective marketing strategy designed to generate maximum buyer enquiry

3 Hot Tips To Get 'The LOVE Price'

1. Ask the agents you're interviewing some key questions that will reveal how they plan to achieve 'The LOVE Price' for your home.
2. Ultimately, this is a business relationship. It's important that you feel 100% comfortable with the agent you choose. Get the specific answers to your questions so you can make a sound decision. Whichever agent you choose, one thing's for certain - choosing an agent, a good one or a poor one to sell your property, will have a lasting impact on your future. The more money you net from the sale, the better off you'll be. You owe it to yourself to undertake sound research and choose wisely.
3. What do you want your agent to do when it comes to negotiating the sale of your property with potential buyers? Frankly, you want them to be able to hold their ground - to sell your property based on its features and benefits - and not on price. It's a truism that an agent who is eager to discount their commission is also likely to be a 'pushover' in the negotiating process with your potential buyers.

CHAPTER 4
COMMUNICATION - ACTING IN YOUR BEST INTEREST

As a coach and mentor to real estate agents all over Australia, I often came across stories of failed agent and seller relationships.

These breakdowns in relationships can be attributed to one or a combination of these five issues:
1. The agent not understanding their seller's 'BIG Why' and not being aware of their concerns or fears about selling
2. The agent is a poor communicator
3. The seller doesn't believe their agent is acting in their best interest
4. The seller feels that their agent has resorted to 'vendor bashing' to get the price down to make a sale and get paid a commission
5. The seller is disappointed in their agent's performance (i.e. lack of results)

Jenny (a pseudonym), an agent from a typical, big 'McDonaldised' agency, called me seeking my advice regarding one of her recent property listings.

It was a property that failed to sell while she had that listing. At some point her principal, out of sheer frustration and concern that the agency may miss out on a sale, took control of the listing. Two weeks later, the principal had it sold, but at what cost?

Needless to say, the original listing agent and the seller's relationship had disintegrated, but the agent had good enough sense to try and learn from the experience.

So what happened? How did the principal get it sold so fast?

I asked Jenny to recount what happened. Here's what she said...

"When I met the two owners to discuss the sale of their home, they seemed really nice. They looked like a loving, happily married couple. I felt they'd be easy to work with. They told me they were selling because they needed more space. It was a great meeting. I left with a signed agency agreement, and commitment to an auction campaign."

Ok, so far so good. "Then what?" I asked.

Jenny explained, "When I left the meeting I bumped into their next door neighbour pottering around in her front yard. The neighbour asked me if I was an agent. I said I was and then she asked me if they were selling. Yes, it's an auction campaign, I responded. That's when the neighbour told me that they (Jenny's new clients) were going through a terribly messy divorce. A 'War Of The Roses' kind of divorce no less."

I asked Jenny what she did with that newfound knowledge.

Jenny said, "I was shocked to hear that they were divorcing. They certainly hid that well from me. I felt that they mustn't have wanted me to know. Maybe they thought by me knowing it would undermine the sale somehow. Or maybe the neighbour had her facts wrong. I decided not to say anything to them about it. I just acted like it was all good and that they were selling to buy a bigger home. End of story."

But it didn't end there.

Over the weeks leading up to the auction Jenny found communication with both owners was falling down. She ended up only ever speaking to the wife throughout the lead up to the auction.

The auction day came, and a reserve was set. Not surprisingly, considering the lack of quality, 'critical conversations' between all parties, the property failed to sell. It turned out only the wife felt informed, the husband had been somewhat excluded from the pre-auction discussions. That left him feeling uninformed, unconfident and somewhat suspicious in terms of where the reserve should be set.

The week after the failed auction, Jenny informed her agency principal about how she'd heard the sellers were getting a divorce and that she'd ignored that information.

The principal encouraged Jenny to place pressure on her sellers using the knowledge of their divorce to leverage a decision to meet the market (i.e. drop their price). But Jenny couldn't. Good for her. She also felt it was way too late to have any kind of open, constructive conversation. That was her fault of course. The reality was she couldn't bring herself to discussing with them what to do next considering the poor relationship she had with the husband.

A few weeks later when the sellers threatened to list with another agency, the principal stepped in and took over the listing. He had a frank discussion with them about their situation. There were tears. This resulted in a dramatic lowering of the seller's price expectations. A sale was made shortly after this. Jenny suspected a great deal of pressure was brought to bear on them by the principal.

Now I can't say with absolute certainty that they undersold the property. It certainly smells of 'vendor bashing' to me and that will always result in underselling. In any case, the poor communication leading up to the auction and post auction wranglings weren't ideal conditions for 'The LOVE Price' to be achieved.

So what should the original listing agent have done?

Well, firstly I think the agent didn't really get the true meaning of what a client-agent relationship is all about. What she didn't appreciate was 'client' means someone who is under their care and protection in terms of the agent being the trusted, professional advisor.

That being the case, the agent should have had a heart-to-heart, frank and open discussion with her clients from the outset of their relationship. She should have made them feel like they could open up and discuss their situation. If she had done that the poor communication between her and the husband could have been avoided.

Were the sellers right in hiding their divorce?

I can understand how a seller could imagine that kind of personal information being used against them (by an unscrupulous agent) in terms of price and getting the property sold.

Sellers have a default defence for this kind of thing - it amounts to: "Whatever you do, don't tell the agent, or it will get told to the buyers." When you read some of the headlines agents use in their advertising like: "Sickness Forces Sale" and "Seller Will Look At Any Offer" it's no wonder sellers are cautious about what they share with their agent.

Paradoxically, being open about your situation with your agent can actually contribute to you getting 'The LOVE Price', because it will help your agent design the best-fitting home selling plan for your circumstances. That's assuming of course the agent you list with is highly experienced and ethical.

Just because a seller trusts their agent and shares sensitive information about their situation doesn't automatically give the agent permission to share it either. Even if the sellers had said it's ok to share this fact about them, the experienced agent would wisely choose what to share and what not to share about the sellers. It is of course their private information, and sometimes what they share about their personal life and their 'BIG Why' doesn't provide any benefit to the seller in getting 'The LOVE Price' if shared.

Of course if the seller had knowledge of detrimental information about their property that may deter buyers, such as, say, the presence of asbestos in the dwelling, that's different.

The agent is compelled to share this kind of information with buyers. Sometimes sellers think it's better to cover up problems about their property, like a shonky car salesman using body filler to hide rust, but actually that can cause even bigger problems in the selling process. Buyers are thorough these days. If there's a problem with the property, rest assured they'll find it. So you're better off pre-empting any objections to your home by allowing your agent to discuss the problem upfront with your buyers.

Your plan then must include great communication, both yours and your agents. Make it a point to select an agent who is an exceptional communicator.

3 Hot Tips To Get 'The LOVE Price'

1. Great relationships are the result of open, frank, truthful, empathetic and caring communication.
2. Not only will you need an agent who's a great communicator (that means they're a great listener too), it's a two way relationship, so you too have to be a great communicator.
3. Don't keep your agent in the dark. Talk to them. Tell them your desires and your fears. Tell them any perceived roadblocks you may be concerned about. Ask them questions. Be open and direct with your answers to your agent's questions.

CHAPTER 5
PRESCRIBING THE BEST PLAN FOR YOU

As you now know, getting 'The LOVE Price' for your home requires the right kind of agent/agency and planning.

The best and most experienced agents will get to know your situation first before prescribing an individually tailored plan to get your home sold for 'The LOVE Price'.

Likewise, you need to include in your plan your selection criteria. Choosing an agent, and how you go about it, can make or break the sale.

I want to tell you a little story about my own experience as a seller when it came time to choosing an agent.

Before I was in real estate, we'd been living in Melbourne for a couple of years. I was the International Trading Manager (unprocessed wool department) for Dalgety.

We owned a lovely 100 year old Edwardian terrace in the inner city suburb of Richmond. We didn't think selling it would be difficult, but wanted it sold quickly to fit in with our plans. We also needed to net as much money from the sale as possible, so getting 'The LOVE Price' was important to us.

CHAPTER 5

We arranged to interview three agents all on the same day because we were in a hurry.

The first agent we met with was very nice. He had a look around our house. Said all the right things. Gave us a sale price estimate. Showed us his impressive results. Told us how he'd plan to sell our home (which was a typical one-size-fits-all plan) and left.

The second agent, well actually there were two of them this time, arrived shortly after the last guy.

These guys were sharp. They arrived exactly at the same time and right on time in separate matching black BMWs. I thought they were cool.

They had a look around our house. Said all the right things. Gave us a sales estimate. Showed us their impressive results. Told us how they'd sell our home (i.e. gave us a sausage machine one-size-fits-all plan) and left.

Minutes later the third agent arrived. He was very nice. Had a nice car too. Had a look around our house. Said all the right things. Then he did something the others didn't...

He asked us, "Why are you REALLY selling?"

So we explained to him all about the wool market crash and how that had affected us. We told him how we were starting a new business back in Brisbane and needed the funds from the sale for seed capital. We told him that we really needed to get it sold quickly to make our move easy.

He then asked more questions. He asked questions about our goals, our concerns, our fears and any perceived roadblocks or challenges we were anticipating with the sale.

I think I did all the talking. This guy was more like a doctor than a sales person. He made it easy for me to open up. His approach felt natural and caring.

The first big concern I shared was around the time-line of the sale. We had to be in Brisbane in 12 weeks' time come what may. Getting it sold and the sale settled before we moved back to Brisbane was important to us.

"That's a very tight schedule" he said. "If it's the usual 60 day settlement, you'll need to start marketing this now."

I asked, "What do you mean now, do you mean this week?"

"Yes," was his blunt reply.

"Oh crap," I thought.

Checking his diary, he worked out a schedule on the spot for the sale. He advised when the first open home would happen and when the first newspaper ad would appear (this was pre-internet days). He set out a timeline for when all the other ads and opens would occur. He booked a date for a pre-auction meeting. He scheduled the day and time of the auction and the expected settlement date.

"It's ok, we can do the first open home this coming Saturday, with the auction on the 4th weekend and that'll mean if it's a sixty-day settlement, you'll have the money from the sale the week prior to your move back home" he said.

"Phew." That was a big relief to know he could get it all done and dusted before we moved back home.

"Any other concerns?" he asked.

"Well, I'm worried how the front of our house looks. Paint's falling off. It looks terrible. I wanted to get it painted before we do the first open home but I just can't see how I can get it done in time," I answered. "Do you think we need to paint it?" I asked.

"Well, street appeal is a big thing in Richmond and the front of your home doesn't do justice to all the renovations you've done inside. For those looking for a renovated terrace, it could be a turn-off," he said.

Our agent (notice how I just called him 'our' agent, that's because at about this point in the conversation I was starting to feel like he was already working for us and not just selling to us) said, "Let me call my painter."

He pulled out his phone, and called his painter.

CHAPTER 5

We could hear their entire conversation, "Yep that's right Tim, we just need you to paint the front of the terrace. It's really not a big area to paint. So just to confirm, if Peter and Karen have the paint ready for you, your team will be here at 8.00am in the morning, you can do that? Great, and you think it'll take just a day, yeah? Awesome. Just hold a second Tim, I'll ask Karen and Peter if that's ok."

With that he pulled his phone from his ear and asked Karen and I, "We can get the front of your home painted tomorrow so it'll look fantastic for our first open home this Saturday, you just need to supply the paint and if you can do that I'll look after the painter's bill. That'll mean we can get an ad booked for this Saturday's open. Are you ok with that?"

What do you reckon we said?

"Yes, let's do it."

We signed the agency agreement and our newly appointed agent left us feeling relieved and excited about the sale.

The house got painted the next day. Not only did they paint the front of the house as they said they would, they also painted our fence which we weren't expecting them to do. It looked fantastic. We felt happy and confident we'd chosen the best agent that suited our needs.

I'm certain it's obvious to you why we chose this agent over the others. It was obvious to us at the time. The third agent made it really easy to choose him. Why? He listened to us, understood what we wanted, understood our motivation and because of that, was able to PRESCRIBE a great, customised SOLUTION.

So it helps when your agent asks great questions. It also helps if you're 100% clear on what you want and what you don't want.

To help you get clear on your plan, here's a list of questions you should ask yourself first before you start interviewing agents to list with. Oh, and by the way, a top agent will no doubt ask you similar questions before prescribing their customised solution for you.

The kind of questions you and your agent should be asking before prescribing the solution:

What's the reason for the sale? What's your 'BIG Why'?
___

What price do you hope to get for your home?
___

Where are you moving to?
___

When did you need to be there by and why's that?
___

When do you need to have the funds available from the sale?
___

Who else is going to be helping you in making the decision?
___

Considering your answers above, out of 10, how would you rate your commitment to the sale? ('0' being absolutely NOT committed; '10' being absolutely 100%, I'm-selling-no-matter-what committed to the sale)
___

Out of interest, why didn't you rate your commitment lower? (e.g. if you rated your commitment 8 out of 10, what was the reason why you didn't rate yourself at, say, 6 or 7?)
___

If you're not 100% committed to the sale as yet, what do you need to do or decide on before you can be 100% committed?

If your home is on the market now - How long has it been on the market? Why do you think it hasn't sold?

What are your biggest concerns (if any) about selling now?

What possible roadblocks could prevent you from getting 'The LOVE Price' for your home?

How would you like to see your sale proceed?

Who are the 'McAgents' in your area? (If you want 'The LOVE Price' your best bet is to avoid the 'McAgents'.)

What are you looking for in an agent? (If you want 'The LOVE Price' you'll need an agent and agency that offers tailor-made, customised service.)

How are you going to select an agent?

Is there anything you don't want in terms of your relationship and dealings with your agent/agency?

Is this about saving money or making money?

If all agents seem the same (the one-size-fits-all agencies will be very similar), how will you make the decision of who you will list with?

What do you know about the agents you've chosen to interview?

When are you looking to select your agent by?

Planning for 'The LOVE Price' - finding the sweet spot

A home selling plan as you can now see is much more than a timeline of actions the agent will take on your behalf: it's a tool for understanding how your home will achieve 'The LOVE Price'.

When you start thinking in terms of making money verses saving money, and custom verses one-size-fits-all, it becomes apparent there's a sweet spot that gives rise to more opportunities to sell for 'The Love Price'.

Sellers who want to 'make money' but choose a 'one-size-fits-all' plan are often disappointed with the result. Sellers who go the custom route but choose the 'save money' plan tend to not think in terms of a premium price, so they can be easily pleased and will generally rationalise what they sold for was what they expected. Sellers who try to 'save money' and accept a 'one-size-fits-all' plan, well, they just expose themselves to shoddy marketing and poor negotiation that usually results in the under selling of their home. However, when you combine a 'make money' plan and a custom service, you put your home into what I call 'The LOVE Price' sweet spot. Here's how that looks...

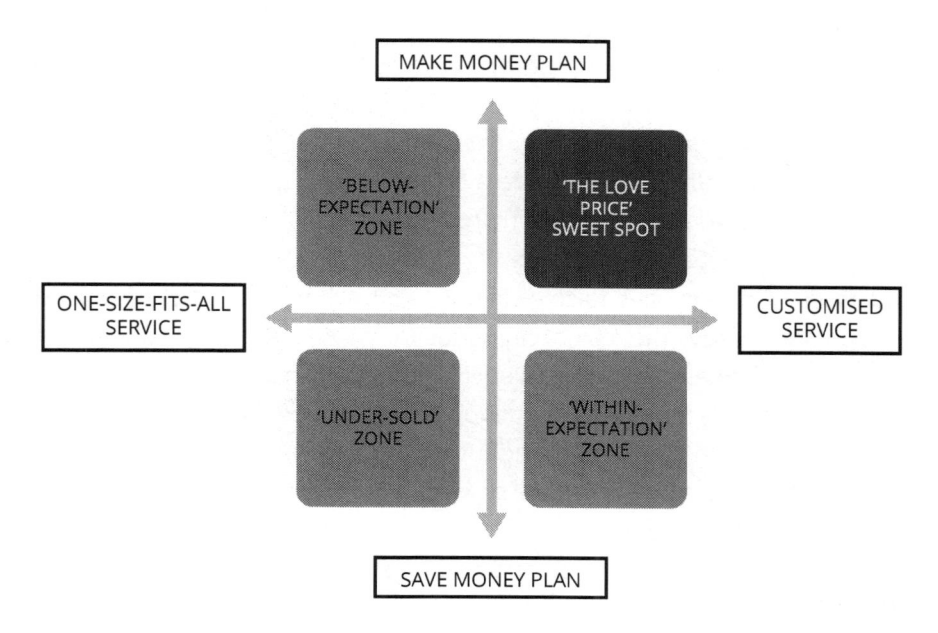

```
                        MAKE MONEY PLAN
                               ▲
                               │
              ┌────────────┐   │   ┌────────────┐
              │  'BELOW-    │   │   │ 'THE LOVE  │
              │ EXPECTATION'│   │   │   PRICE'   │
              │    ZONE     │   │   │ SWEET SPOT │
              └────────────┘   │   └────────────┘
                               │
ONE-SIZE-FITS-ALL ◄────────────┼────────────► CUSTOMISED
    SERVICE                    │                SERVICE
                               │
              ┌────────────┐   │   ┌────────────┐
              │ 'UNDER-SOLD'│   │   │  'WITHIN-  │
              │    ZONE     │   │   │EXPECTATION'│
              │             │   │   │    ZONE    │
              └────────────┘   │   └────────────┘
                               │
                               ▼
                        SAVE MONEY PLAN
```

4 Hot Tips To Get 'The LOVE Price'

1. An experienced agent will ask you similar questions about your situation during the interview. By having considered these questions first, you'll be in a better position to have a more valuable conversation with each agent throughout the interview process.
2. Be open and direct with your agent. You'll want them to be open and direct with you too.
3. Interview three agents before you decide who to list with. But who do you choose? The tendency will be that you'll want to interview the most familiar. That's ok provided you interview one or two agents who'll provide a contrast. In any case, ensure you include at least one agent from a quality, boutique agency who offers a customised service.
4. Beware of agencies falsely claiming to be 'boutique'. Just because an agency says they're boutique doesn't make it so. Just because an agency is small and independent (i.e. not in a franchise group) doesn't automatically make them boutique either. My definition of a boutique agency is - "A small independent agency that offers a high quality, made-to-measure real estate service to a discerning clientele." There are franchise groups now starting to claim (in part or in full) to be boutique. To me franchise and boutique are at the opposite ends of the spectrum. If it walks like a duck, quacks like a duck, guess what? It's probably a duck. That's all I have to say about that.

STEP 2: **PRICE**

Of all the things home sellers want to know, it's "What price am I going to get for my home?"

At the end of the day, selling your home comes down to an exchange of money doesn't it? Sure it does. It's all about money. It's about getting a price that helps you move on with your life.

That's why you often hear agents say, "Selling your home for most people is singularly the biggest financial transaction you'll make in your life."

When it comes to getting the best price for your home, the 'Buyer's LOVE Price' no less, how you derive your price and then express it to the buying public is a major determinant of your success.

In this section of the book we'll discuss why the way you express your (asking) price often gets in the way of 'The LOVE Price'. I'll show you why price stops most properties from achieving 'The LOVE Price'; and I'll show you pricing strategies that you can use to ensure you get 'The LOVE Price' for your home.

CHAPTER 6

THE 6 DYNAMICS THAT INFLUENCE THE 'SOLD PRICE' OF YOUR HOME

Every home seller wants to know how much their home is worth. Right? Of course they do. It's understandable. I have to say though, many have an exaggerated expectation that agents should know exactly what their property is worth, nearly within a few thousand dollars or so of what it'll sell for.

The reality is, despite the availability of up-to-date historical sales data from property information services like 'CoreLogic RP Data' and 'PriceFinder', agents can still get the price wrong. Why is that?

It has a lot to do with the 'price dynamics' at play at that point in time. These dynamics, some obvious, and some not so obvious, have an influence on the price that a property sells for.

Ask your typical big ego agent and they'll tell you they're the 'NO.1 INFLUENCE' on the 'sold price' of your home.

Yeah right.

It's just not that simple. There's more to it than that.

Sure, your agent will have an influence on what your home will sell for. Certainly NOT the only influence though and frankly they're NOT always a good influence either.

Here's why...

There are actually **'6 DYNAMICS THAT INFLUENCE THE SOLD PRICE'**. They are:

1. The property seller's motivation
2. The property buyer's motivation and the type of buyer they are
3. The market trend on the day of an offer or bid being made
4. The presentation of the property and degree of WOW factor
5. The quality of the marketing of the property
6. The agent's ability to negotiate

These 6 DYNAMICS all have a BIG role to play in the final outcome. They are all equally important. As each of them can vary, in some cases quite dramatically, so can the sold price. When you get so many variables affecting price, the possibilities are enormous, making the outcome less predictable than what many agents would have you believe. The fact is, with so many variables at play, **similar properties often don't sell for similar prices!!**

To me this is the elephant in the room. It's why so many agents just don't get the price right in the first place. It's why sellers find it hard to work out what their home is worth and it's why 'price' is so subjective.

What that means is, you can have two very similar properties located in similar streets, even the same street or the same apartment building, and because just one of the six 'PRICE-INFLUENCERS' was different for one of the properties, so was the sold price.

Here's an example of what can happen. Let's say you list your property for sale...

Your agent provides a pretty thorough market appraisal, identifying all relevant recent sales.

On paper the properties identified in the 'COMPARATIVE-MARKET-APPRAISAL' make good sense. They all seem to be similar properties to yours. "A good indicator of the sold price you can expect," your agent will say.

But hang on a second. Have you considered the '6 DYNAMICS' that may have influenced their sold price?

Probably not. Because unless your agent sold those properties, he or she probably doesn't know. Even if they did sell all of them, they still may not know because most agents lack the knowledge and often subtle distinctions to see the dynamics at play.

For example...

- One of the comparison properties may have been sold under some kind of 'SELLER DURESS' (e.g. the seller had lost their job and had to sell quickly)
- Another of the comparisons may have had 'poor marketing' and as a result didn't get enough exposure to the market or attract enough of the right 'A-BUYERS' (I'll explain who these 'A-BUYERS' are later in the book), causing the property to be 'UNDER-SOLD'
- While another had its sold price botched because the agent wasn't a competent, skilled communicator and negotiator.

This is why getting an 'APPRAISAL' is fraught with danger.

You can't just simply say... "Oh, there's a property that just sold like mine, so I can expect what they got."

That assumption doesn't take into consideration the '6 DYNAMICS THAT INFLUENCE THE SOLD PRICE' and how each of those dynamics affected the sale of the property you're using as a comparison and as a 'PRICE-GUIDE' for your property.

Now you might be thinking this makes pricing your property hard. You're right, it does make it hard.

CHAPTER 6

Any agent that waltzes in and pumps out their chest professing to know exactly what your property will sell for either doesn't understand the '6-PRICE-INFLUENCERS' and the affect they can have on the sold price or they're psychic. (Not many psychic agents out there so I'm guessing they're the former.)

So what's the solution?

Well, the first thing to do is find an agent that's more concerned about getting you 'The LOVE Price' than trying to 'estimate' what your property is worth. (Did I say estimate, I mean guesstimate.)

Secondly, make sure your agent provides you with a detailed Comparative Market Appraisal of your home, but make sure it's realistic.

3 Hot Tips To Get 'The LOVE Price'

1. Ask the agents you're interviewing for a realistic 'COMPARATIVE-MARKET-APPRAISAL' and only view it as a guide, not some hard and fast fact that you can bank on.
2. Don't automatically assume the agent who professes to know exactly what your home is worth will get you the best price.
3. Always remember the adage, "Similar properties often don't sell for similar prices!!"

CHAPTER 7
HOW REALISTIC IS YOUR PRICE?

The BIGGEST MISTAKE you are likely to make as a home seller is not being realistic in terms of price and how quickly your home will sell. It's not your fault. You're human after all. We humans have a tendency to overestimate or underestimate things, and when it comes to establishing a price for your home, you don't want to be making decisions based on a false reality.

The truth is, it's hard for sellers to be realistic about the price. That's not just me saying that, it's science. There's a little-known phenomenon economist call **"The Endowment Effect"** also known as 'divestiture aversion' which causes sellers to think their property is worth more than what the market is willing to pay. (Source: economist Richard Thaler, 1980)

The Endowment Effect is a measure of perceived value. Research conducted by Cornell University concluded that a person's ownership or attachment to something increases their perceived value of that thing. In other words, home sellers are always going to have an inflated view of their home's worth because of their attachment.

Sellers also tend to look at price from the point of view of either what it owes them, or what they need from the sale. They wrongly assume they can work out what it's worth by simply adding up what they paid for it plus what they spent on it, plus an added (guesstimated) amount for how much better their home is compared to the neighbour's house that just sold.

Remember also, similar properties often don't sell for similar prices. So looking at what your neighbour sold for may be completely irrelevant to what your property will sell for.

So how can you avoid 'The Endowment Effect' and establish a realistic price as a guide for the sale of your home?

Start by considering these questions...

a. Have you seen any property like yours sell in the area in the past six months?
b. If you said yes, how much did it/they sell for?
c. What's happened to the market since then?
d. What's the current market trend and what will that do to the price over the coming months?
e. Did you actually inspect the property/properties that sold?
f. If you said yes to the last question, how did it/they compare to your home?
g. How much more or less was it/were they in terms of price compared to yours? (Remember the 'endowment effect', so try not to let that influence you and be as objective as possible.)

Your next step is to find an agent who can give you a realistic 'Comparative Market Appraisal'.

Just to be clear, I don't want you to think an appraised price, as realistic as it may be, will in any way increase or decrease the chances of you getting 'The LOVE Price'. It's not about that.

The main purpose of a 'COMPARATIVE-MARKET-APPRAISAL' is to give you a guide. It'll also help you avoid over-pricing or under-pricing. But most of all, it'll give you a benchmark price to aim for and to beat.

For this reason, a REALISTIC or CONSERVATIVE form of comparative market appraisal is your best option.

Here's how your agent should conduct a realistic 'COMPARATIVE-MARKET-APPRAISAL' of your home...

1. Ask your agent to compile for you a complete list of reasonably comparable properties that have sold in your area in the past six months. When I say 'reasonably comparable', if you're selling a house on say, 400m2 of land, the list should only contain sold properties on a similar amount of land, give or take. If you're selling an apartment, the list should contain similar sized apartments (e.g. if your apartment has 3 bedrooms, the list should only contain 3 bedroom apartments. Also look at the square metres of each, they should be reasonably similar). Make sure the agent doesn't censor this list. At this stage the longer the list the better.
2. Get them to list all similar properties to yours that are on the market now. This will help you gauge your competition. Don't underestimate the influence these competing properties will have on your price. Buyers will be comparing yours to them. (When building this list, ensure your agent doesn't censor what goes into it other than ensuring the properties listed are 'reasonably comparable' to yours.)
3. From the list of sold properties, identify all the properties that are similar to yours but for some reason aren't quite as good (e.g. poorer maintenance, no swimming pool, poorer location). In other words, your home should sell for more than them. Mark these 'worst'.
4. From the list of sold properties, identify all the properties that are very similar to yours. Try and establish three properties that are very similar to yours (especially in terms of how your buyers will perceive it). Mark these 'likely'.

5. From the list of sold properties, identify all the properties that are similar to yours but for some reason are better than yours. Mark these 'best'.
6. Based on what you've selected, you can now estimate a realistic appraisal range for your home's worth. You'll end up with three prices. Worst case, likely case and best case. Often, I'll even identify a range for the 'likely case' scenario (e.g. $750,000 to $775,000).
7. There's one other price to consider and that's the 'dream price'. From the 'best case' examples, select the most expensive property that is 'reasonably comparable' to yours (but let's be honest, it's probably better in some way) and mark that as a possible 'dream price'.

Ok, so now you have a realistic appraisal ranging from 'worst case' right up to a 'dream price'. But please don't forget that the property market is dynamic. What that means is, it's always changing, and although we're trying to be objective about this, your realistic appraisal is still going to be somewhat subjective.

WARNING: 'Local agents' can become a little bit insulated from what's happening in the marketplace in other areas. In some ways it's possible for local agents to influence price simply because they convince their sellers they know the market better than anyone else. That can put a cap on prices. It's like a self-fulfilling prophecy.

The moral of this warning is simple really. Don't automatically assume the local agent knows the price better than an 'out-of-area' agent.

From the moment you receive your 'realistic' comparative market appraisal to the day your home is placed on the market, prices can change. So the next thing to consider is the market trend. We'll cover that in the following chapter.

2 Hot Tips To Get 'The LOVE Price'

1. A 'realistic market appraisal' should include 'worst case', 'likely case' and 'best case' scenario prices your property may achieve if sold within the same market trend.
2. Don't automatically assume the 'local' agent has a better handle on price. Sometimes, 'out-of-area' agents have a better chance of getting you 'The LOVE Price' because they're more open to possibility.

CHAPTER 8
THE MARKET TREND IS YOUR FRIEND

"What do you think is happening to the property market over time?" Do you know? What real evidence do you have to support your answer? Lastly, what impact is that going to have on your sold price?

These are critical questions that address the trend of the property market. You'll need to answer them before you decide on the price you hope to get and can reasonably expect for your home. Your answers will also have an impact on the method of sale you choose.

Here's the thing... after selling nearly 1,000 properties, I've come to realise the MARKET TREND IS YOUR FRIEND!!!

Let me first explain what these market trends are. Specifically, there are **'3-MARKET-TRENDS'**:

1. The market is either 'TRENDING UP' over time – that means there's proof that the market is rising; and therefore it could be described as a 'SELLER'S MARKET', or...
2. The market is 'TRENDING FLAT' over time – that means all the evidence is saying the market isn't going up or down, it's just bouncing along without much change, or...

3. The market is 'TRENDING DOWN' over time – that means all the evidence is pointing to prices easing or even dropping; in which case it's commonly referred to as a 'BUYER'S MARKET'.

Knowing what the 3 Market Trends are should make it a little more obvious why I say "THE MARKET TREND IS YOUR FRIEND." Let me spell it out just in case...

It's because when you know what the trend is, it doesn't matter so much what the realistic 'COMPARATIVE-MARKET-APPRAISAL' price of your home is, what matters is you now know what to do to beat the trend or even benefit from the trend. That's why it's your friend. It helps you win against it, no matter what it's doing.

For example:
- If it's 'TRENDING DOWN' – the quicker you sell the better; that is, the longer your property stays on the market the less it'll be worth
- If it's 'TRENDING FLAT' – what's important is to get it sold before it becomes stale - in a flat trending market, the longer the property's on the market, a stigma develops and buyers start to ignore it. That will cause the price to be driven down over time
- If it's 'TRENDING UP' – an up-to-date appraisal makes even more sense. That is, over time the price will go up. Now that will also depend on the time frame. In this case you will want to take advantage of an upward trending market by NOT capping the sales price at a pre-conceived idea of what it's worth as it could be worth more than you or your agent thinks

WARNING: Most sellers get caught up in the hype of selling their home and nearly always believe the market is going up or about to go up. Most sellers also believe their property is worth more than it is. That's human nature. Desire (fantasy) replaces reality.

It may be the case that at the time of you reading this book the market is indeed trending up. If that's so, you need to ask this question...

"By what percentage per month is it going up, and how long will that upward trend last?"

Don't fool yourself into believing markets go up and up forever or stay flat, or go down forever. You and I both know they don't.

I learnt that when I was a commodity trader for Dalgety, selling wool all around the world. As a wool buyer and trader you soon get to know a lot about market cycles. You learn how a booming market will always end up busting at some point. You learn that markets that are flat eventually boom. The truth is, you tend to learn these cycles the hard way. Now that's ok when you're playing with Mr Dalgety's money. But when it comes to selling your home, suffice to say, you'll want to avoid miscalculating what the market is going to do next. I've seen too many home sellers miscalculate the market trend. Ouch!!

You have to consider the impact the economy will have on the property market in the near future. You also have to look at the bigger picture. Look at world economic trends as they too can have an impact on the market over time.

You need to understand what's driving the current trend in order to determine what the market will be like in the near future. The question to ask is how sustainable is this trend? How long will it last? These are all good questions to ask your agent. Your agent should be an expert on 'MARKET TRENDS'.

3 Hot Tips To Get 'The LOVE Price'

1. Don't try to "crystal ball" the market. Be guided by the facts. Sellers often reject buyer's offers because they think the market is about to go up and sadly, often sellers who gamble on the market going up, lose.
2. The best way to safeguard against markets going up or down is to sell and buy again in the same market.
3. Picking the top or the bottom of the market is one of the hardest things anyone can do. At best it's a guess. My suggestion is to consider long term trends instead of trying to identify the market top or bottom.

CHAPTER 9
DAYS ON MARKET - THE LETHAL STIGMA

I have a question for you...
    "What are the two things you think about a property that's been on the market for a long, long time?"

Genuine property buyers invariably answer with, "It's either OVER-PRICED" or "There's something WRONG WITH IT".

That's what twenty years in real estate and speaking to thousands of buyers over the years has taught me.

Pretty much every buyer out there thinks the same way when it comes to a property that's been on the market a long time. That's why excessive 'days on market' generates what is basically the BIGGEST and most UNWARRANTED, NEGATIVE PERCEPTION buyers can have about your home.

Please hear this, any NEGATIVE PERCEPTION buyers have about your home, even though it may be completely unwarranted, will make it very hard for you to get 'The LOVE Price'.

The longer your home stays on the market unsold, the greater the STIGMA (i.e. negative perception) of it being over-priced or something wrong with it, grows. That stigma grows and grows and grows until it becomes a self-fulfilling prophecy, causing your property to be bypassed by ready-to-snap-it-up, motivated property buyers. Guess what impact that has on your home's price? That's right. It artificially pushes your price down. You don't want that!!

Here's the other thing... this STIGMA occurs quicker than you think.

It starts to grow around week five of a property being 'on the market'. (When I say 'on the market', I'm referring to a property that's been 'exposed' to the market via channels like the internet, signage and newspaper advertising.)

Most of the ready-to-buy, motivated property buyers will look at your property between week one and week three of it going on the market.

If you haven't sold it by week five or six, you have a big, big problem on your hands.

Here's why...

There are 3 TYPES OF BUYERS. One you'll want. The other two will waste your time. Here's a brief description of both...

'A-BUYERS' are your BEST buyers. Here's a list of their attributes:

- They're ready, willing and able to buy now. That means they're well-researched. It also means they're now 100% committed to the move. It also means they've spoken to their bank if borrowing money and have their finances in order
- Being 'ready, willing and able' means they're in a good position to make a positive 'BUYING DECISION'
- An 'A-BUYER' will often make a buying decision within 30 to 60 days of reaching the point of being 'ready, willing and able' (provided stock levels of property on the market are normal)

- 'A-BUYERS' focus predominantly on new listings coming onto the market, while being less receptive to properties that have been on the market for what they perceive as being a long time (i.e. 5 weeks or more)
- When your home is listed on realestate.com.au and/or domain.com.au, the DAYS ON MARKET clock starts ticking (every week that goes by without receptive 'A-BUYERS' inspecting your home, the less likely it is that they'll inspect or buy your property)
- The majority of 'A-BUYERS' take a rational approach to their buying decision to begin with. Or at least that's what they try to do
- The trick is NOT to give them a 'rational reason' to overlook your property
- Losing these 'A-BUYERS' is where the STIGMA starts to set in

'B-BUYERS' are basically tyre-kickers. Here's a bit about them:

- 'B-BUYERS' are in 'RESEARCH-MODE' and because they're still trying to understand values and working out what they want and what they can and can't afford, they're usually not ready to make a 'BUYING DECISION'
- 'B-BUYERS' tend to look only at properties that are within their budget and often they'll focus more on property that's in the lower range of their budget
- Their research is influenced largely by their conservative budget
- The vast majority of people looking at property online are 'B-BUYERS'
- At an auction, 'B-BUYERS' will rarely register as a bidder. However if they do, because they're not totally ready to buy, they may open the bidding but they won't go beyond the lower end of their budget.

Their bid will be low and it's unusual for them to bid further once another buyer enters the bidding.

'C-BUYERS' are the vultures. This is how you can recognise them:
- 'C-BUYERS' tend to be cashed-up investors looking for a bargain property to add to their investment portfolio
- They're hoping the seller is desperate to sell and their goal is to buy well below the market
- They tend to be very rational/analytical in their buying decisions
- They have extensive market knowledge which they intend to use to their advantage
- They are rarely first home buyers as they tend to be seasoned property buyers
- They make low-ball offers/bids

Understanding and targeting the right buyer is just part of it. But before you can make an informed decision about which 'method' of sale is best for you, you need to consider how you can avoid the DAYS ON MARKET STIGMA. Singularly, the best method for getting 'The LOVE Price' for your home must take into consideration days on market and targeting the best of the three buyer types.

The solution comes in the form of attracting the highest number of 'A-BUYERS' to your property in the first one to three weeks of your property being on the market.

Here's why...

If you don't attract 'A-BUYERS' you'll be left with only 'B-BUYERS' who aren't ready to buy because they're just in 'RESEARCH MODE' and they're really just 'tyre-kickers'. Regardless of what method you choose, you'll invariably attract some 'C-BUYERS.' How you can avoid these buyers relates more to the promotion of the property which we'll discuss later in the book.

CHAPTER 9

Let's say you finally realise you're expecting too much for your property by week five or six; well unfortunately, it'll be too late, all your 'A-BUYERS' and even your 'B-Buyers' will have moved on by then and goes without saying, the 'C-BUYERS' will be circling like vultures at this point.

It's funny, over the years I've heard sellers who are struggling to sell say this... "Won't they just make an offer despite what our asking price is?" Mostly they won't.

They either don't perceive the value in your property, or they've become disheartened by how much you're asking for it. Or the property simply isn't what they want.

This is why days on market can be so lethal.

If you want to get 'The LOVE Price' for your home, you must avoid the days on market STIGMA. The ONLY way you'll do that is by triggering an emotional, HOT-BUTTON response in your buyers so they act sooner. In the next chapter we'll look at the first step you can take to avoid the STIGMA.

3 Hot Tips To Get 'The LOVE Price'

1. The longer a property takes to sell, the less likely you'll get 'The LOVE Price'.
2. Days on market is THE biggest roadblock a seller faces. If you want the best price for your home, in most cases, 'The LOVE Price' sweet spot is in the first two to three weeks your home is on the market.
3. If your home has been on the market for more than six weeks without receiving a reasonable offer or bid, you need to consider withdrawing the property from the market to give it a fresh start with a new agent. Alternatively, your agent needs to 're-position' the property (if he/she knows how) so that it attracts a new group of buyers whose expectations match what your property offers. Don't assume 're-positioning' automatically means dropping the price either. I'll be discussing how you can 're-position' your property in several different ways later in the book.

CHAPTER 10
THE PRICE DETERRENT

Avoiding the days on market STIGMA will save you big time. It's all about attracting enough A-BUYERS early on.

There are two things to realise about days on market.
1. Days on market is directly related to price; and
2. Days on market and your buyers' perception of value are connected

What I mean is, as soon as you put a price on your property you draw attention to it. The listed 'asking price' in the case of the private-treaty method of sale is one of the main indicators buyers use to determine if your home matches their buying criteria.

If the listed 'asking price' is in their budget they'll look at it. If it isn't, and especially for well-researched buyers, they'll ignore it. In the case of a property being advertised without a price (i.e. auction), the same still applies in terms of where the property appears in an online property search. That is, even without a price, property portals such as realestate.com.au and domain.com.au, require the agent to allocate a (hidden) price that will be used to set search criteria (more on this later).

The warning here is, buyers eliminate properties that they assume they cannot afford.

Price then is often a 'DETERRENT' for a buyer making an initial enquiry. They won't even attend the open home if they think the seller is wanting too much, or in other words the property doesn't represent value for money.

The price you place on your property could be stopping the right buyer from looking at it.

Your best buyers will inspect your property when it's new to the market provided the price doesn't scare them away and provided you've done everything possible to 'maximise buyer enquiry'.

If you haven't sold it by week four or five, many buyers viewing your property will automatically assume it's either over-priced or there's something wrong with it. Right?

So the wrong listing price is a HUGE deterrent in getting 'The LOVE Price' for your home. The longer you wait to address this deterrent, the longer your home will stay on the market and at some point that STIGMA grows.

Ok, so how do you avoid the price deterrent so you can achieve 'The LOVE Price'?

Let's revisit what exactly is 'The LOVE Price' so that we can start talking about how you can achieve it for your home.

The (Buyer's) LOVE Price is a 'Premium-Price' or quantifiable 'High-Price' that's the result of a highly-motivated A-BUYER, who is 'ready-willing-and-able' to buy, falling in love with your home and deciding they absolutely MUST own your property. That's when a buyer will become 'EMOTIONALLY-MOTIVATED'. They stop thinking with their 'head' and start following their 'heart'. They imagine living in it one day. They become attached to your home. They have to own it. They don't want to lose it, so they'll compete to get it and this is what drives up the price of your home.

When someone is 'EMOTIONAL' about a property, when they fall in love with it, they want that property so badly that they can become a little irrational about it.

Every property I've ever purchased, I can honestly say I fell in love with it within minutes of inspecting it. Love's funny that way. You just know it's the one, right? And when that happened, I would want that property really badly. Money would start to burn a hole in my pocket just itching to be spent. I'd think to myself, "This is the one, this is it, this property is mine." And as they say, the rest is history. I'd make an offer and do everything I could to buy the property.

Over the years I've learnt that I'm not alone when it comes to falling in love with your dream property.

It's not unusual for an 'EMOTIONALLY-MOTIVATED' buyer to spend right up to the top of their budget. But it doesn't mean they'll stop there either. This 'heightened state of desire' often results in buyers throwing their budget out the window which leads them to paying much more than they had initially planned; in some cases it causes them to rob their piggy bank (i.e. borrow to the max).

The bottom line is, experience has shown me that 'EMOTIONALLY-MOTIVATED' buyers will pay more for something if they fall in love with it and want it badly enough.

Researchers at Duke University who study how the brain values things - a field called 'Neuroeconomics' - have found that your feelings about something and the value you put on it are calculated in a specific area of the brain. They found that buyers who fall in love with, say, their potential new home, probably wouldn't pay as much for it if they could resist their emotions.

So 'The LOVE Price' happens when a motivated 'A-BUYER' falls in love with your home. They go from thinking 'rationally' about the purchase to not being able to resist their emotions. It's their emotions that drive the price up and this only occurs when you remove or lessen the 'PRICE-DETERRENT'.

THE LOVE PRICE

When you remove or lessen the 'PRICE-DETERRENT' you attract rational buyers who fall in love with your home. Their emotions cause them to think less rationally about price and that's what causes the price to go up (and with the right marketing and negotiation strategies it'll go up even more - I'll show you how to do that later in the book).

The other thing is this - the most emotionally-motivated buyer is often the one that just missed out on another property (e.g. another buyer outbid them at an auction). They won't want to miss the next property that they fall in love with.

OK, you should be thinking...

"I want to get 'The LOVE Price'. I want a buyer who's not resisting their emotions and who's emotionally-motivated to buy my home."

If you want 'The LOVE Price', your pricing strategy and sales method must be designed to elicit an 'emotional response' within your buyer audience. The starting point to do that is by removing or lessening the 'PRICE-DETERRENT'.

If that doesn't excite you, it probably means you just want a 'quick sale' and are happy to take the first price, that is sell to an unemotional buyer who'll offer you a 'rational price' and that's OK if that's where you're at.

But if you want your sale to benefit from emotionally-motivated buyers then listen up...

All you have to do is employ a sales method that removes any possible 'PRICE-DETERRENT' and maximises 'A-BUYER' enquiry in the first three to four weeks of it being on the market.

The 5 Goals of Removing the 'PRICE-DETERRENT'

1. Attract as many 'A-BUYERS' as possible whose 'BUYING-CRITERIA' matches your property and get them to inspect your home within the first 3 weeks of your home being on the market. That's the premium-price sweet spot. Those first 3 weeks on the market is where you'll find your most motivated buyers.
2. Attract 'A-BUYERS' that value your property the most. To do that your marketing must depict all the best elements of your property. Show your property in its best light. The better your marketing, the easier it is for the right buyers to recognise your property as a great match for them. This is about attracting motivated buyers who'll fall in love with your home.
3. Avoid confusing, misleading, or driving your best 'A-BUYERS' away. By removing the 'PRICE-DETERRENT' you allow the qualities of your property to dictate to them if it's worth a look. Pricing should never get in the way of attracting your best buyers. Every aspect of your marketing (and that includes the pricing strategy), MUST attract 'A-BUYERS', not repel them.
4. Place pressure on them to act. Motivated 'A-BUYERS' who fall in love with a property tend to feel greater pressure to act sooner and make an offer because of the fear of loss. When someone wants a property badly enough, they won't hesitate.
5. Place pressure on them to pay a premium price. Psychology studies have shown that 'EMOTIONALLY-MOTIVATED' people will pay more for something if they want it badly enough. By removing the price deterrent, your right buyer/s will do what it takes to buy your home.

CHAPTER 11
CHOOSING THE BEST METHOD OF SALE

The big question now is, what method of sale will you use? And what 'asking price' will you list your property at so as to avoid the price deterrent to NOT ONLY get it sold but to also get 'The LOVE Price' for your home?

Drum roll please... this is how you do it...

THE BEST METHOD'S GOAL: Attract as many 'A-BUYERS' as possible whose 'BUYING-CRITERIA' matches your property and get them to inspect within the first 3 weeks of your property being on the market.

HOW TO REMOVE THE 'PRICE-DETERRENT': You can either go to the market with 'no price' (e.g. an auction) or ensure your 'asking price' (i.e. 'list price') is not a deterrent and elicits offers and gets buyers to the negotiation table fast.

The 'wrong pricing' will only confuse, mislead, or drive them away. Going in with a high price will deter buyers. Going in with no price or a low asking price will attract more motivated buyers to view your property. (Don't worry, this isn't about under-quoting or under-pricing, all will be explained further in this chapter.)

GETTING IT SOLD: You need to place pressure on your buyers to act. That'll happen if motivated buyers fear losing the property by not acting fast enough. The 'fear of loss' is another powerful emotional-motivator.

Without it, buyers will be slow to make a decision and you don't want that.

A buyer who perceives the value in your property will automatically assume that there will be other buyers out there who'll also perceive similar value. They'll feel the pressure of competing. Their fear is that they'll lose the property. This will result in a serious buyer making an offer sooner rather than later.

Ultimately the best **METHOD OF SALE** all boils down to a pricing strategy. So let's consider your pricing strategy options.

Generally speaking you have **3 PRICING STRATEGIES** to choose from...

1. **Private Treaty 'TOP-DOWN-PRICING' Strategy** – this is where there's an actual asking price, like say, $750,000. This version of setting your 'asking price' produces a sales result usually below where you start.

    But don't fall for insidious over-pricing tactics!! It's often a mistake to list your home with an agent purely on the basis that their market appraisal of your home was the highest. While it's true that you can always 'come down' in price if your home doesn't sell, there are many other factors you should take into account.

    The market is always looking for new listings. That's why for example realestate.com.au has a button to list properties newest to oldest. This means that for the first few weeks your home is on the market, it will generate more inspections than at any other time. All the buyers in your price range will rush to see your home. Those that have been looking for some time are the ones who've done their homework and are ready to buy now. They will however also be the most aware of the true market value of your property.

THE LOVE PRICE

Just as sellers take the attitude 'we can always come down', buyers think they will wait until the price drops. You'll often find that a property that receives an offer, for example, $1,370,000 when first placed on the market, may become 'stale' and only attract bids of $1,200,000 after being on the market for too long (that's exactly what happened to another agent's vendor). That's because the longer your home stays on the market, the more buyers feel they have negotiating power.

If your home is correctly priced it will make buyers feel they need to snap it up before someone else does. However, if the price is too high, they feel no such sense of urgency.

2. **Private Treaty 'BOTTOM-UP-PRICING' Strategy** – This is where the property's advertised asking price is expressed for example as either… "Offers from $X" or "Offers over $X" or "$X +".

With a 'bottom-up-pricing' strategy, what generally happens is the price goes up (as opposed to down in the case of the 'top-down' strategy).

The 'bottom-up-pricing' strategy works because the price deterrent has been lessened. In other words, because the price is expressed as, say, "Offers over $700,000" the right 'A-BUYERS' will quickly recognise the value in the property and consequently will be attracted to inspect it.

To establish where to set the 'bottom-up' price you'll need to have had a realistic market appraisal prepared for your home. The 'bottom-up' price should reflect somewhere between the 'worst case' scenario price you could expect and the 'best case' scenario price.

For example: let's say the property has been appraised with a worst case to best case range of $700,000 to $770,000, the 'bottom-up' price could be expressed as either "$700,000+" or "Offers over $700,000". This example has a 'worst case' price that's about 10% below the likely case price. In some markets/properties that'll be too low. So as an alternative, consider setting your "Offers over" price at around 5% below the 'best case' price provided that's also in line with your realistic appraisal.

No surprise, it's the lower end of the range that entices buyers to inspect your home. Once inside your home, one or more of these 'A-BUYERS' will recognise the full value of the home, fall in love with it and move to the negotiation table. (Remember, it's not where the negotiations start that's important, it's where they end up that counts - more on that in the negotiating chapter later in the book.)

OK, so you're probably thinking... "If the 'offers over' price is set too low, won't that attract buyers who'll only want to pay the lower end of the appraised range?

Well, possibly yes. There could be some of those buyers. But there will also be 'A-BUYERS' who are looking at the key features such as location, address, maintenance, interior design, number of bedrooms, bathrooms and land area to name the main 'buyer-criteria-features' and of course, the price.

So you'll be attracting all types of buyers, including 'A-BUYERS' who are well-researched and ready to buy. Your best buyer will assign the greatest value to your home and will be more inclined to pay the upper end of the appraised range, or even beyond it depending on supply and demand for similar properties and the level of competition.

The goal of 'BOTTOM-UP-PRICING' is to get a lot of buyers to your open home, create a real buzz, with the expectation that amongst the many buyers inspecting your property, one or more buyers will fall in love with your property and become an 'EMOTIVE-BUYER'. They are the kind of buyer that goes to the top of their budget and sometimes over it.

We want rational 'A-BUYERS' because up until they looked at your home they will have been looking at properties within the lower end of their budgeted range. Guess what? They won't be as nice as yours. It's human nature to be disappointed with what we can afford. We often want more. Such is the case with rational buyers.

The good news is, by the time they see your home, several of them will have seen enough properties to know that if they want to get what they love, it's probably going to cost them a little or a lot more. Some of them (especially those who aren't resisting their emotions) will be up for that.

The main difference of the 'offers-over' approach as opposed to using a 'fixed price' is that there is nothing in an 'offers-over' approach that prevents them from looking at your property. They'll have hope. We want them to have hope, hope that they can afford your property, hope that no one else wants your property and hope that your property will be their next home.

There is one other BIG DIFFERENCE in this approach most agents won't explain to you. When you go from bottom up, there is no artificial ceiling blocking how high your property can sell for. Enough reason alone to choose this approach over the traditional 'top down' private treaty method wouldn't you agree?

Now, just to be absolutely clear, I'm NOT advocating 'under quoting' or 'bait advertising' or any form of misleading marketing for that matter. Not only is that wrong, it's just not smart. Your 'bottom-up' price should reflect the price that is no lower than the lowest end of the realistic, comparative market appraisal range you received for your property.

Also, we must remember recent concerns (mostly in New South Wales and Victoria) about consumers being misled and losing money on due diligence (e.g. a building and pest report or a bank valuation) as a result of dubious 'under quoting', is generally in relation to property being sold at auction.

With an auction, buyers invest in various forms of due diligence prior to the auction. If an agent 'under quotes' to a prospective auction buyer, that buyer may end up wasting money on due diligence on a property that they can't afford to buy (i.e. it sells at auction above the quoted range). I get why that's bad.

Private treaty however is different to auction. With private treaty a buyer can make their offer to purchase the property conditional on due diligence being conducted after a purchase price has been agreed upon by both buyer and seller. Private treaty then is not prone to under quoting issues when it comes to buyers wasting money on due diligence.

3. **Auction 'No-Price' Strategy** – This strategy can work even better than the 'bottom-up' strategy for some properties/areas especially where demand outstrips supply. With no price at all, the price deterrent has been removed altogether.

This maximises the number of 'A-BUYERS' inspecting the property in those crucial first few weeks of being on the market.

Some of the buyers may even (wrongly) think they'll get themselves a bargain at auction. You know what? That's ok, provided they weren't misled into believing that. We want as many 'A-BUYERS' inspecting the property as possible. Then we want as many registered bidders at the auction as possible vying for your home. This creates a competitive environment and competition between two or more 'A-BUYERS' drives up price.

Again, your agent shouldn't 'under quote' or mislead buyers in terms of price. New laws in Queensland for example strictly prevent quoting a price or price range for properties being sold at auction. I can't say I agree with that totally, but the law is the law. I recommend you check the laws in your state before authorising your agent to quote a price. (Note: in Queensland, your agent is permitted to provide buyers with a copy of your 'COMPARATIVE-MARKET-APPRAISAL' report with your permission of course.)

THE LOVE PRICE

Imagine your open home abuzz with enthusiastic buyers. Imagine auction day with multiple bidders all vying for the property. That's where auctions come into their own. Because auctions are really just a way of bringing the negotiations out in the open, buyers will feel the pressure of competing for it against other buyers. The more they want it, the fear of loss kicks in and they'll tend to compete for it even harder. It only takes one buyer who fears missing out on the property to kick the price up.

The objection that some sellers have with this method is that not all properties sell under the hammer. That's true. But it's just one day in the life of the campaign. The goal remains the same. Get as much action happening on the property before the days on market stigma kicks in. You have to look beyond auction clearance rates and look at the average days on market the auction method produces.

Generally speaking, days on market with auctions is less than any other method of sale and that's a good thing.

It needs to be said though, a typical 'McAgent' will try to convince you that the BIG difference between the 'bottom-up' method and auction, is that the date of the auction acts as a deadline. They'll say an auction deadline provides buyers with an added incentive to get their things in order, like arranging finance pre-approval. However, this isn't strictly true. A love-struck 'A-BUYER' is by definition 'ready, willing and able'. They don't need a deadline. If they love your home, they'll be ready to buy it now. The benefit, if any, of a deadline is that any love-struck 'B-BUYERS' who are on the verge of becoming an 'A-BUYER' will be forced to be ready to bid on the day.

So which method works best?

Well, often that depends on the area and the type of property. There's no hard and fast answer here. I'm not fixated on which is the best method other than it must REMOVE or LESSEN the PRICE DETERRENT full stop. I will say this, **supply and demand** for properties similar to yours will have a major influence on the effectiveness of the auction method. Obviously when demand is high and supply is limited, there are more buyers competing for property. An auction needs that public showing of competition. Without it, auctions can fail.

The bottom line is, the method is just one piece in 'The LOVE Price' puzzle. There's more to getting 'The LOVE Price' than the method alone. (We'll cover those in steps 3, 4 and 5 in the following sections of the book.)

But do you know who is fixated on there being only one right method?

That's right, the 'McAgents'. They're completely fixated on what they say is the best method. That's because they're stuck in a process. Remember, they're running a real estate burger factory. That means one-size-fits-all. That means process before individual needs and attention.

However, your property, your area and you, may be better suited to one method and not the other.

When it comes to getting 'The LOVE Price', all I can say at this point in the book is, you must remove or lessen as much as possible, the 'price deterrent'. That means either going with the 'bottom-up' method or an auction 'no-price' method.

5 Hot Tips To Get 'The LOVE Price':

1. Emotionally motivated 'A-BUYERS' are less price sensitive in terms of staying within a budget as a rational buyer is. Herein lies the HUGE advantage 'BOTTOM-UP-PRICING' and Auction 'NO-PRICE' methods have over the 'TOP-DOWN' FIXED-PRICE strategy.
2. The 'TOP-DOWN' method encourages 'pay-less-than-the-asking-price' thinking with no limit to how much less the price can drop - away from 'The LOVE Price'.
3. Both the 'BOTTOM-UP-PRICING' method and Auction 'NO-PRICE' method encourage 'pay-more' thinking with no limit to how much more the price can go - towards 'The LOVE Price'.
4. When a seller prices their home too high, not only are they unnecessarily extending the days on market, causing the 'over-priced' or 'something wrong with it' STIGMA, their high price is actually helping their competition to sell.
5. By using a sales method that removes the price deterrent, you'll be attracting more motivated 'A-BUYERS' to your open homes and to the auction. This creates a buzz about the property, placing pressure on the buyer or buyers who've become emotionally hooked on your home.

CHAPTER 12

YOUR AGENT JUST DOESN'T 'GET' PRICE VARIATION STRATEGIES

If you choose to sell your property by the 'fixed price' private treaty method, sometimes a variation in the 'list price' of your property is necessary.

The 'list price' is the advertised 'for sale price' of your property.

Now, if you've engaged an inexperienced (or dare I say it, unskilled) agent who chooses the wrong time to vary the 'list price' – or to even neglect making a variation when it's really necessary – it's fraught with danger.

There's an optimum time or circumstance to vary the 'list price' of a property and it's a decision that shouldn't be taken lightly. That optimum time is prior to the days on market STIGMA occurring.

To gain an understanding of the decision-making process, you need to know a little about the 'life cycle' of a real estate marketing campaign.

Here's what often happens...

When your property enters the market for the first time, it's as if a light bulb is switched on over the heads of the 'A-BUYERS' whose 'buying-criteria' matches your property. It's like... "Bingo, we have a match!!!"

The moment that happens in the mind of a motivated, ready-to-buy 'A-BUYER', they suddenly become aware that there's a very real possibility that other buyers will like your home too. They become somewhat more motivated to get in fast to check your property out. They'll be hoping and some even praying that your home is 'THE ONE'. This hope also generates fear. Fear that they may get gazumped by another buyer and potentially miss their opportunity to buy your property.

That's why in those early weeks of marketing, competition for your property is at its most intense.

It's most likely that at this time, genuinely motivated 'A-BUYERS' will make the highest offers on your property. After all, they won't want to miss out on it, owing to competition with other eager buyers.

But what happens if you're underwhelmed by early offers or worse still, receive no offers at all in the first few weeks?

As I've said in earlier chapters, the first 3 or 4 weeks of your marketing are crucial. No offers in this period should be ringing alarm bells.

In all honesty, at this stage it may be necessary to look at the possibility of varying your 'asking price'.

This is another area where the value of having a brilliant real estate agent on your side can really pay dividends.

It's crucial that you don't leave it too late to vary the asking price and here's why...

The longer your property is on the market at a consistent price, the more likely it is that interest will fade away until your property is perceived by an increasingly savvy marketplace as either unwanted or over-priced. That's the STIGMA that grows on all properties over time. Qualified buyers lose interest and move on to other properties in the marketplace that are more realistically priced.

When this happens, the potential for selling at the best price will evaporate before your very eyes.

CHAPTER 12

The BIG WARNING here is: if you haven't sold by week 5 of being 'on the market', that is, having had 5 solid weeks of advertising your property, there will be a growing STIGMA on your property that it's either over-priced, or there's something wrong with it. Buyers' perception is everything and once they have this perception about your property, it is very difficult to change their mind about it. The mud sticks.

There's a simple self-evaluating rule I've utilised for many years that helps home sellers determine the best time to vary their asking price.

I call this rule the 'No Offers Rule'.

There's a couple of things I need to explain about the 'No Offers Rule' before you leap in and use it.

There are two conditions that must be met before this rule can be applied.
1. The property must be well presented (preferably decluttered and styled by a professional)
2. The property must be professionally marketed (preferably using both the internet and print media) to attract the attention of all current prospective buyers in your home's price range. (I'll be talking more about marketing and property promotion in Step 4 of this book.)

You'll see the rule contains a list of marketing criteria and enquiry activity benchmarks (below). Please understand, every area is different. The rule below reflects the market I work in. You'll need to discuss with your agent what works best in your area in terms of each of the 'criteria' and 'benchmarks' listed. So please look upon this list that forms the 'No Offers Rule' as merely a guide. In other words get advice from an agent in your area that gets how this works before you start adjusting your price on your own (you don't want to make a mistake with this as that could lead to the under-selling of your home).

Here's the criteria/benchmarks I use in my area:
- Two advertisements and no response (i.e. no offers in writing); and/or
- Over one thousand 'internet buyer views' and no offers; and/or
- Two 'A-BUYER' second private inspections at your home and no offers; or
- You have received 'low-ball' offers but have failed to attract an offer close to your asking price. 'Low-ball' offers are often a symptom of an over-priced property; or
- When open home inspections are falling short of five groups at each open.

Your agent should be meeting with you every week to discuss marketing and enquiry activity. In addition to the usual reports your agent gives you, at one of these meetings, but no later than day fourteen of the marketing programme, they should provide you with a review of the progress of the marketing in terms of eliciting a good offer. At this meeting it would be wise to at least consider the 'No Offers Rule'.

BUT WHAT IF BUYERS AREN'T GIVING YOU FEEDBACK?

Silence is NOT always golden when it comes to selling your property.

What I mean by this is, sellers often confuse 'no offers' or 'no price' feedback from buyers as an indication that either the agent isn't doing their job right (i.e. encouraging buyers to make an offer regardless of the list price) or the magic 'right buyer' hasn't come along.

The only REAL feedback that's worth paying attention to are written offers. Not verbal offers. Verbal offers need to be disregarded as they're NOT genuine feedback because they don't indicate the true motives of the person making them. So anything other than written offers in terms of feedback is questionable and may mislead you.

The reality of receiving no feedback on price or offers is that it's usually because the buyers that are currently inspecting the property (online or at open homes, etc.) have a different expectation of what they'll get for their money.

That is, a buyer's initial enquiry on a property is usually based on a limited amount of information. Buyers tend to use just three pieces of information to make their initial selection before enquiring further on a property advertised (i.e. clicking on the 'more details' button in the case of the internet, or in the case of print media ads, checking the property out online).

The '3 Pieces of Information' are: specification, price and photos ('Specification' includes property type, location, number of bedrooms, bathrooms and car parks etc.)

In the case of the 'FIXED PRICE' private treaty method of marketing, the list price is really no more than a flag or indicator to the buyer that there's a potential match. So the list price is merely a marketing tool. The price says to the buyer... "Hey look at me, I'm in your budget and you can afford to buy me."

Now that the buyer has flagged the property as a potential fit, they'll inspect it with a degree of hope and expectation.

If however the property turns out not to be a perfect match, no offer will be made nor will they provide feedback on price. Even if they did provide feedback on price, their feedback is not valid because they're actually looking for a different property to yours.

The only expert on price is the A-BUYER that's a 100% perfect match for your property and who is well-researched and 'ready-willing-and-able' to buy now.

When a buyer turns their back on your property what's actually happening is, they have a greater expectation of what their money will buy.

THE LOVE PRICE

In other words, they don't 'perceive value' in your property. In most cases it's not a matter for these buyers putting in a lower offer; the property is simply not suitable in their view, so they walk away from it.

Now referring back to the **'No Offers Rule'**; if after several open homes no offer is forthcoming, it indicates that the price is attracting the wrong sort of buyers whose expectations don't match what your property offers.

At this point you have 3 options...

a. You could do nothing and wait for either the right buyer to appear or the market to increase - however it's best to consider the 'MARKET TREND' at this point. Think about what waiting does to 'BUYER PERCEPTION' (i.e. "What are the 2 things buyers think about a property that's been on the market a long, long time?" - Their answer is usually... 'over-priced' and/or 'there's something wrong with it'); or

b. You could invest more money into advertising the property. Consider pictorial print media advertising at this point if you haven't done so already - "Print and digital are an essential media mix to reach property buyers. Three-quarters of buyers with a personal income of $100,000 or more use property content from newspaper publishers to decide on their biggest lifetime purchase. Around half of all prospective buyers who use news media real estate web sites also read print sections. Real estate advertisers reach the highest earning property buyers using newspapers, with this group 33% more likely to read newspapers than the general population. Among prospective property buyers in general, newspapers rank second only to magazines." (Source: Simon Batty, The Newspaper Works and Enhanced Media Metrics Australia data); and/or

c. Look at an adjustment to the price as this will most likely place the property in front of more buyers with hopefully a matching expectation in the current market. When it comes to deciding how much to vary the price, think in terms of percentages. A reasonable percentage change in your asking price is usually between 5% to 10%. This will re-position the property so that it grabs the attention of a new group of 'A-BUYERS'. If you vary the price by less than 5%, in most cases you'll be wasting your time because that small change won't help to present the property to different buyers whose expectations are a better match for your property.

But what about auctions?

The above applies to an auction also. The only difference being there is no 'list price' as a guide for buyers.

Instead, buyers can be given a 'Property Report' ('COMPARATIVE-MARKET-APPRAISAL') which details three comparable properties that have sold within the last three to six months in your area. The three properties are meant to be indicative of the price that may be achieved for your property. (Of course you as the seller would need to approve of the three properties included in the report.)

So let's say the price of the three indicator properties are turning buyers off your property. If that happens you would review the three properties and replace them with properties that are a better indicator of what your property may be worth. The trick here is to choose three properties that are a very good match with your property but also match buyer perception of value.

Whatever you do, don't try and manipulate the market by including properties in your report that are better than yours. You'll only turn buyers off your property because they'll believe you have an inflated view of what your home is worth.

Hot Tip To Get 'The LOVE Price':

1. If after three weeks on the market you're not getting genuine offers in writing from buyers, you need to discuss that with your agent. It's no good thinking that a buyer will eventually make an offer if you wait long enough. The longer you wait, the less likely it is you'll get 'The LOVE Price'.

STEP 3: **PRESENT**

My Mum, Judy Hutton, is a well-known interior decorator. Growing up as the son of an interior decorator you learn a thing or two about home presentation. (I think the bedroom I shared with my brother was the tidiest, best decorated boy's bedroom in the world - we didn't have any choice though, LOL.)

In the 1980's through to the early 2000's my Mum's business boomed. This was despite the fact that interior decorators were often seen as a nice, luxurious, yet unaffordable investment by many home owners. For those that struggled to come to terms with paying for a decorator's advice, my Mum would point out, "Good taste costs no more than bad."

Most home owners today appreciate the importance of presentation when it comes to selling property. We have many TV shows like "The Block" to thank for that. But when it comes time to sell their own home, many still back their own judgment, opting to style their home themselves (or make no changes at all), instead of paying an expert to do it for them.

Maybe it's because they don't see the value in spending money on styling their home prior to selling it? Maybe they don't see how improving the presentation will have a positive impact on the sale price? Maybe they think their real estate agent knows all there is to know about styling and will point them in the right direction? Maybe they believe styling is expensive and they're just trying to save money?

THE LOVE PRICE

The reality is, there is no saving by not investing in styling. A poorly presented home will cost you dearly. If your taste in interior decoration doesn't match those of your ideal buyer, you could lose thousands of dollars. The problem is, most people's idea of how a home should be presented for sale is largely subjective. It's based on their own personal taste, and has little to do with maximising your home's presentation to get you a high price.

If there was just one thing you learn from this section, I hope for your sake it's 'presentation sells'.

That being said, this section of the book will take you through the 'presentation' step in getting 'The LOVE Price' for your home.

I should say, this chapter deals with the full extent of presentation; from styling your home, to capturing the best qualities of your home in your photography, right through to presenting your home to the public (i.e. at open homes).

CHAPTER 13
THE WOW FACTOR!!

I really like the Toyota Prius Hybrid because of its fuel efficiency (3.9ltr/100km). What's not to like about that?

Buuuuut...

The Mercedes Benz E300 BluTEC Hybrid with its not too dissimilar fuel efficiency (4.3ltr/100km) has a way bigger WOW Factor.

And it's that WOW factor that has such a BIG, BIG impact on the price people are willing to pay for something.

Similarly for residential property, WOW and 'The LOVE Price' go hand-in-hand.

It's all about perception of value. This is often why similar properties can sell for vastly different prices. It's often because one property had the WOW factor and the other didn't.

Look, please don't make the mistake and think that WOW can only happen for expensive, luxury properties, or for properties with an amazing view, or some other unique or coveted feature. That's simply not true.

In all price points, in all areas, there are some homes that have the WOW, and many others that don't.

WOW is what gets 'A-BUYERS' to act sooner. WOW ignites emotional-momentum towards your buyer making a buying decision. Actually, WOW can have an instantaneous effect on your A-BUYER.

Have you ever bought a property where the moment you lay your eyes on it or walked in the front door you knew you'd found your next home? In that moment, the heart starts pumping quicker. Your imagination is unleashed, filling your mind with all the possibilities of how you'll live there. Have you experienced that?

I certainly have and in that moment you've bought the property (figuratively speaking).

That's what WOW is and does to an 'A-BUYER'. It's where price, features and benefits meet perception of value and the desire to own the property.

Ok, so maybe you're thinking your property doesn't have the WOW factor, or maybe hasn't got as much WOW as you'd like. Don't worry. As I said, in all price points you can have WOW even without those intrinsic WOW factors like great views or the like.

Here's the good news - WOW can be manufactured. How? Well, simply by lifting a property's presentation beyond the competing similar properties in your price point.

So imagine you have a two bedroom apartment that you want to sell. Let's also say there are three other two bedroom apartments with similar outlooks and at a similar price point for sale in your building. This actually happens a lot. Your apartment has exactly the same finishes, fixtures, features and benefits to the other three apartments that are competing with yours. So how do you compete under those circumstances?

Most agents will say the only way to compete with similar properties in similar locations, is price.

Now in some ways that's very true. Remember, you'll need to avoid the days on market STIGMA, and you'll do that by removing or lessening the price deterrent. That'll certainly get buyers inspecting your apartment before the competition's. However, when buyers are presented with a lot of choice, removing or lessening the price deterrent will help to get them in the front door but they'll still be comparing it to the other apartments available.

Getting 'A-BUYERS' in the front door is step one in getting 'The LOVE Price'. Step two is to set your apartment apart from the competition. But not by discounting. The smarter way is by adding WOW.

That's the opportunity here. By creating WOW in comparison to the competition properties, you set your home apart. Combine that with removing or lessening the price deterrent, the groundwork will be laid for your buyers to come to the negotiation table sooner. That's how you get 'The LOVE Price'.

The simplest, most direct and affordable way to add WOW, is done by improving your home's presentation. Presentation can easily be improved on virtually any property by professional styling.

Presentation sells!!

Back in my property development days when I was the Director of Sales and Marketing for an award-winning residential development company, we quickly worked out that fully-furnished display apartments that were professionally styled to demonstrate the lifestyle qualities of our properties had a direct impact on the price we could sell them for.

The better the styling, the better the presentation, the bigger the WOW, the higher the level of attachment, the higher the price we'd achieve. Ka-ching!!

There's no doubt, presentation, WOW and 'The LOVE Price' are all linked.

Now it's not just me saying this. There's been numerous studies on property buyer behaviour and what influences their purchasing decision. One such study by Clare E. Branigan and Cathal Brugha, titled "Behavioural Biases on Residential House Purchase Decisions: A Multi Criteria Decision-Making Approach", found women were most influenced by "how the property looked" or "the feeling" it created; and it went on to reveal that these influences were stronger than the monetary issue of "Is it good value?"

When you consider women account for 91%* of all new home purchasing decisions, Branigan and Brugha's findings are all the more relevant when it comes to presentation and the WOW factor in terms of achieving 'The LOVE Price'. (*Source: Stephanie Holland, She-conomy.com, President/Executive Creative Director, Holland and Holland Advertising.)

In another study, titled "Residential Real Estate Purchase Decisions in Australia: Is It More Than Location?" published by Southern Cross University's Business School, results of their buyer survey further confirms how important presentation is. This study investigated the factors that prospective buyers consider when purchasing residential property. They found that even more than features, views, location and affordability, the thing that influenced the decision to purchase a property the most was maintenance and interior design.

These findings and my own observations and experience say presentation and WOW sells!!

2 Hot Tips To Get 'The LOVE Price':

1. The simplest, most direct and affordable way to add WOW, is done by improving your home's presentation (which includes maintenance). Presentation can easily be improved on virtually any property by professional styling.
2. The better the styling, the better the presentation, the bigger the WOW, the higher the price that can be achieved.

CHAPTER 14
WHAT AGENTS DON'T TELL YOU ABOUT DECLUTTERING AND STYLING

It's exciting to think how much emotionally-motivated buyers will be prepared to pay for your home isn't it? After all, you've seen other properties in your neighbourhood sell for prices well above what you paid for yours.

Before getting too excited though, have you considered how you'll feel if people actually offer less than your expectations?

Well, fortunately for you as you've now learnt, getting 'The LOVE Price' is made much more achievable by uncovering the WOW in your home.

But Be Warned: Most if not all agents aren't really qualified to help you create the WOW factor in your home. Sure they can suggest you do a little bit of 'decluttering'. Maybe they have an idea or two around presentation. It's not their job other than to encourage you to employ a professional stylist. Oh, and some agents like to think of themselves as having the skills to be both agent and stylist. That should concern you if they do. Are you employing a 'stylist' or an agent to sell your home? Do you want a jack-of-all-trades who is a master of none, or do you want a master of each skill being used? (Hint, you'll be better off with a master of real estate marketing and sales.)

'Decluttering' and 'styling' need a well trained eye and someone with not just a flair for interior decorating but someone who has been trained in the art of styling for the purpose of selling property.

'Decluttering', in simple terms, means opening up spaces so your property appears larger and more accommodating.

'Styling' however, is about presenting your home to appeal to the most likely buyers.

Note that I've said, "Appeal to the most likely buyers". It's not necessarily about making your property resemble a glossy home magazine pictorial. Rather, it's about understanding the marketplace and the kinds of buyers demanding property such as yours, then appealing directly to them.

When buyers take 'emotional-ownership', that's when price becomes less of an issue to them. So the key is to make your property feel comfortable to the prospective buyer – let them take emotional ownership as early as possible.

With the right combination of decluttering and styling, you'll be able to overwhelm buyers with a 'gotta have it' emotional pull. That's the WOW factor in essence.

The key is a balancing act between achieving a WOW presentation and yet remaining neutral enough so potential buyers can see themselves owning it.

Many sellers find this balancing act quite difficult to achieve on their own. However, like many things, the process can be helped with the guidance of an objective, experienced eye.

When choosing an agent, ask if they can introduce you to a decluttering and styling professional that has achieved outstanding results for their clients, time after time.

CHAPTER 14

The reason for choosing a 'property styling' service as opposed to an interior designer or interior decorator is that property stylists are dealing with the important task of preparing sellers' homes for sale day in, day out. They have first-hand, up to the minute knowledge of what buyers are looking for – it comes from listening to comments from real estate agents every single day.

Here's how my wife and business partner, Karen Hutton, one of Brisbane's leading property stylists explains it...

"Initially I'll meet with you at your property and discuss all of the features and benefits that will appeal to likely buyers. I'll get a strong feel for the kind of person that's likely to buy it.

In some cases I'll recommend we keep all the existing furniture, but simply move some pieces into new positions. We've been able to create a whole new energy closely matching the profile of buyers with this simple step.

In other cases we've agreed to putting part or all of the existing furniture in storage, and hiring pieces that will instantly allow potential buyers to feel at home and 'take ownership' of the property.

You see, to put the WOW into a home, it often comes down to taking the "you" out of your home. What I mean is, all those personal keepsakes that you love may not be actually helping your buyer feel at home.

The thing to always keep in mind is that you aren't presenting your home to appear in a glossy magazine or win any beauty contest – you're presenting your home for a very specific purpose - and that's to make it irresistible to the buyer who will fall in love and buy your home for a premium price.

It's always a collaborative process and the results are always worth the effort." (You can find out more about Karen at http://karenhutton.com.au/.)

Getting Your Home Ready For Sale

Creating just the right first impression is accomplished in the overall look of your home, but it's also very much in the details. Potential buyers start to form an opinion of your house before they even walk in your front door. For a house, the street appeal is a BIG determinant. That includes things like the landscaping and your home's façade. For an apartment it's a little different, it happens the moment the front door opens. What will they see first? What impact will that have on them? These are key questions to answer.

It's important to maximise first impressions, but then you must also carry that same attention to detail right through the rest of the home.

Your goal is to romance potential buyers. You want them to lose their hearts and say, "This is home. We have to have this house!"

In a national survey carried out by homegain.com, they found that out of the 12 things you can do to your property to prepare it for sale, the top two ways to increase your home's worth in the eyes of your buyer was simply a 'clean and declutter' followed by 'styling'.

And remember:

"Buyers are not looking to buy property! What they're really looking to buy is a better life (property just happens to be the way they'll get it)."

For the presentation of your home to really attract buyers (and the highest offers) you need to make buyers want what you've got - give them a glimpse of a better life and you'll be that one step closer to getting 'The LOVE Price' for your home.

The good news is, you can present virtually any property so that it has the WOW factor (if you know how to do it).

Recently, I was contacted by the owner of a large ground floor luxury apartment in New Farm. The apartment had been on the market for several months with another agent in the area. During that time, not a single offer in writing had been received. I understand from the sellers, there was one buyer willing to offer $1,000,000 but a written offer was never forthcoming. Understandably, the sellers were frustrated.

When I conducted a realistic market appraisal of their home, the appraisal range we agreed upon was actually no different to what their former agent had told them. So, in my opinion, the sellers had realistic expectations.

I found out that the previous agent did the old one-size-fits-all plan. They had it listed at a fixed, 'top-down-price' of $1,295,000; and they did numerous open homes. But no written offer and no sale.

What excited me about this apartment was the large living space and its great courtyard. It just didn't present as well as it could. There was no WOW. So I felt it needed a little styling magic. Enter my stylist wife, Karen.

Karen started the transformation off by decluttering it. That resulted in the owners putting thirty boxes of their personal things into storage along with several bookshelves, rugs, some musical instruments and a sleeper sofa. Talk about WOW, decluttering really opened up the space inside. Next was the courtyard. This was the real hero of the property but it was empty and looked unused. So Karen brought in a groovy outdoor setting and repositioned the owner's outdoor dining table and pot plants. Inside the apartment a breakfast nook was created, furniture adjusted to create a better energy flow and bedrooms were joojed. By the time she was finished, the property was virtually unrecognisable compared to the state in which the previous agent advertised it. It now had a definite WOW factor. Once that was done our photographer did a great job capturing the WOW that Karen had created.

Just four days into the promotion of the apartment we secured a cash offer of $1,250,000 which I negotiated to a successful sale. The result? A sold price of $1,300,000.

That was $5,000 higher than what the previous agent was advertising it for. I should also point out, the sold price was more than the appraised 'best case scenario' price. The seller was over the moon.

2 Hot Tips To Get 'The LOVE Price'

1. The agent you choose should be able to recommend a professional decluttering and styling service by a qualified stylist with real-world real estate styling experience.
2. Regardless of what you and/or your agent feels about your property in terms of presentation, always get a second opinion from an experienced professional stylist.

CHAPTER 15
THE HERO SHOT - CAPTURING WOW!!

Now that you've decluttered and the joojing of your home has been completed by your stylist, it's time to capture the WOW.

I'm talking about photographing your home. In particular capturing the WOW factor in a single photograph which we call the 'Hero Shot'.

The Hero Shot is that one photo that will cut through the marketing noise of competing properties to capture your buyer's attention.

The Hero Shot needs to be as attention-grabbing as possible. This is where communication with your photographer is key.

Your agent should have a 'brand style guide' to brief their photographer on the style of photography that will make your home stand out online and in print.

The hero shot can be a close up. It's ok if it doesn't tell the whole story of your home. It's not about documenting the entire property. It's about capturing a feeling. It's that feeling which will connect with your buyer.

The hero shot has to show lifestyle, and portray your home in a positive way. We want it to look real. Natural. Liveable. Not fake like a show home. So don't 'over-style' for the photo shoot. What I mean is, don't go and set up a dining table with your best china dinner setting. You don't want the hero shot to be over-staged.

Tips for the best hero shot:

Always use a professional photographer, no matter how inexpensive the property is.

Key images are the living areas, kitchen, view and the exterior.

Express the theme of the home in the hero shot. Ask yourself, "What's the core attraction of this property?" Think about why you bought the home. What 'sold' you on it?

Twilight images can really enhance your listing. The most amazing shots can be taken during 'the magic hour', when the sun is setting and the sky turns that deep blue. That's when you'll get the most vivid colours in the sky, interior and exterior, and really see the details in the property's own lighting. There's a psychological reason behind why people's imaginations are captured by twilight photography. You see, primitive man sought shelter for the evening as the sun went down – they would light their fire and settle in for the night. Photographing a home at the magic hour draws on thousands of years of primal need. Modern man also relates the twilight hour as a time to go home, settle and relax. Make use of this little-known psychological fact in your photography.

Make sure your agent's photographer is using top equipment.

The quality of the photographic equipment is the key to clarity, colour saturation and the brightness of the images.

Some photographers digitally add in brightness after the shot has been taken to enhance it. This results in poorer quality images. (But sure, they would be better than those taken by your agent's own camera. Even so, I don't recommend these 'enhanced-afterwards' shots.)

Your photographer should have these items of equipment to take premium images:
- Wide angle lens: These allow photos that make rooms look large and spacious without distortion or unrealistic proportions.
- A tripod: A pro photographer would never use a hand-held.
- An off-camera flash: A pop-up flash simply won't cut it. This is one of the most important tools in real estate photography.

Ok, so we've covered styling your home in the previous chapter and now in this chapter capturing the WOW in your photography to use in the 'promotion' of your home. But there's one other aspect of the 'presentation' step that is usually overlooked.

I'm talking about your open homes. Sure that's something your agent takes care of, but there are things you and your agent will need to do to in terms of presentation that'll ensure your opens are a great success. In the following chapter I'll be discussing the 7 deadly sins of open home presentation.

3 Hot Tips To Get 'The LOVE Price'

1. Express the theme of the home in the hero shot. Ask yourself, "What's the core attraction of this property?" Think about why you bought the home. What stood out in your mind when you first inspected the property?
2. The hero shot has to show lifestyle, and portray your home in a positive way. We want it to look real. Natural. Liveable.
3. The hero shot captures the WOW. But make sure it's the WOW that your ideal buyer can relate to.

CHAPTER 16
THE 7 DEADLY SINS OF OPEN HOME PRESENTATION

The 'open home' is possibly one of THE most important steps in selling your home and getting 'The LOVE Price'.

Now, you may be wondering how anyone could actually stuff up an 'open home'. The reality is, it's where many agents fall down.

Think about it. The 'open home' is like the stage for the selling of your property. The moment the open home 'a-frame' sign is placed on the footpath out front of your home, it's show time!!

So 'open home' equals 'show time' and that means you have about 30 to 45 minutes to impress the hell out of your buyers. It's about showing off your home's WOW. Without the WOW, there's little chance you'll move your buyers out of the 'realistic-rational' buyer group into the 'emotionally-motivated-smash-the-piggy-bank' buyer group.

The open home is about moving your buyers towards making a buying decision. For that reason, your open home needs to be conducted with all the finesse of a choreographer.

Everyone has a bad open home story. Seems to be a common topic at dinner parties these days. But it's not entirely the agent's fault.

CHAPTER 16

Both agent and seller have a hand in the success or failure of the open home.

Over the years I see pretty much the same seven open home mistakes happening. Each mistake erodes the emotional-momentum and buyer confidence that is much needed to move your buyer/s to a buying decision.

Avoiding these 7 mistakes will go a long way in you getting 'The LOVE Price' for your home. So let's take a look at them now...

THE 7 DEADLY SINS OF OPEN HOME PRESENTATION:

1. **Not 100% Clean** - there's absolutely no point opening your home up to the buying public unless your home is absolutely spotless inside and out.

    Seems like balconies, verandahs, decks, courtyards and poolside areas get a second rate clean compared to the home's interior living spaces. BIG mistake.

    It'll suggest your home's external entertaining spaces are a dirt trap. That's a BIG turnoff to buyers. I see this happening a lot in apartments.

2. **It's a 'HOT' House/Apartment** - no, not hot as in stunningly stylish, but hot as in all the windows were closed, air-conditioning was off, ceiling fans were off and it's like a sauna inside. This is easily fixed.

    On those warmer days, make sure windows and doors are open, ceiling fans are on (set to a gentle speed), and in key areas have the air-conditioning going. Remember how nice it is walking into an air-conditioned shopping centre in the height of summer to escape the sweltering heat? Imagine your buyers having a similar experience, they won't want to leave. Your agent needs to allow enough time to set all of this up.

3. **Too Many Teddy Bears** - no I'm not kidding. One time I inherited, from another agency, a luxury block of apartments to sell.

   They'd been on the market for several months with the other agency without a sale. The apartments definitely had the WOW factor but the WOW was being smothered by the overly staged styling the developer's decorator had done.

   For example: one of the bedrooms had about fifty stuffed teddy bears on the bed. Ok, you got me, I'm exaggerating, but you get the picture, it looked ridiculous and was one of many 'styling' mistakes that was distracting buyers' initial impressions. Not only that, the styling 'positioned' it to the wrong buyer profile.

   The lesson - remove all distractions, keep it simple, present the open home to the level your targeted, ideal buyer aspires to live. Oh, and by the way, I sold all six apartments in under sixty days at full price. Presentation sells!!

4. **'Where's the Agent?' Syndrome** - ever arrived at an open home to find the agent is nowhere to be seen? Unfortunately, it happens all too often.

   For many agents, and especially those that don't cap the number of listings they take on board, they're so rushed on Saturdays going from open home to open home, it's easy for them to arrive late.

   You'd agree, that's not the best way to greet your buyers. It gets worse. The late agent now has no time to properly prepare the home. So its presentation will suffer.

   Also, what these agents tend to do, is let the queued up buyers into the home while they go around the home opening doors and windows.

   This leads to missed opportunities in the form of buyers sneaking in and out before they can be registered. No registration means no follow up can be made.

5. **"It's ok, My Assistant Will Do The Open"** - that's what busy 'McAgents' say to their sellers (or maybe don't tell them that's what they plan to do).

   That sounds a little cynical, maybe it is. You be the judge. Go and check for yourself the number of open homes on a Saturday in your area where the agents who listed the property aren't actually the ones doing the open.

   I visited an agent's open home of a multi-million dollar apartment recently and the listing agent wasn't even there. Instead, one of his sales associates manned this amazing property all on their own. I was shocked.

   Your listing agent is your best bet for an amazing open home. No one is going to be as enthusiastic and passionate about your property as your listing agent will be. They also will have more intimate knowledge about your home. When it comes to getting 'The LOVE Price', a knowledgeable agent is absolutely crucial.

6. **The Atmosphere Is Dead** - well I reckon this is one of the biggest mistakes. What I'm talking about is, you want there to be an amazing atmosphere for all of the buyers inspecting the property. This is created in several ways.

   Firstly, it's about getting enough buyers to the property so that buyers feel the buzz of interest in your home. There's nothing worse than a "ghost-town-open-home". That'll give buyers the impression no one else is interested in your home. Buyer perception is everything. If your open home only has a dribble of buyers inspecting it, they'll not feel that buzz and leave deflated or worse, expect a bargain as no one else is interested.

   A great atmosphere can also be created through the use of our senses. For example, sound. If it's so quiet in the open home that you could hear a pin drop, that's going to make for an uncomfortable experience.

We want your buyers to relax. Let down their guard a little, and feel at home. So turn on some music. Keep the sound level just right, not too high, not too low.

Another sense we can appeal to is smell. Get your home smelling clean and fresh, maybe even yummy. The old cake baking trick is a little clichéd, but scented candles work well and create a relaxed atmosphere.

Consider handing out cool refreshments to your guests, especially on warmer days.

Here's another idea (which I've done and it works amazingly, especially for a home that has a gourmet kitchen) - bring in a chef at the open home to do a cooking demonstration. Talk about great aromas plus it will really captivate your buyers.

There's lots you can do to amp up the atmosphere. Make sure spaces are bright and not dark and dingy. Strategically turn on lights and lamps. Open curtains and shutters. If your home is affected by western sun, ensure showing times take that into consideration.

Just remember though, the one-size-fits-all mistake. Your open home needs to be staged to fit well with the kind of buyer who'll love your home the most.

7. **Clock Watching** - this is the other downside with an agent who lists more properties that they can handle personally themselves.

Here's the thing, they'll tell you they can handle all of their listings because they have assistants to help them with their opens. I think that's a great idea. But what I'm talking about is when a listing agent can't hang around at the end of an open to talk to an eager buyer because their Saturday open home schedule is full. Their tight schedule places pressure on them to leave on time to ensure they get to their next open on time.

Ok, so they can follow up that eager buyer later in the day when time permits. In my book, that's a BIG mistake. You've got to strike when the iron's hot so to speak. Your agent's open home schedule needs to have sufficient gaps in between opens so that eager buyers can receive the attention they need to move them to a buying decision.

By the way, I recommend 30 minute opens and the agent should leave an hour gap between opens to provide plenty of time to assist those eager buyers, some of which will gladly go to contract straight after an open. That means the maximum number of opens an agent can do really well is around four or five on a Saturday.

Of course there are other factors that will make or break your open home. But they're more to do with the 'promotion' of the property and the sales 'pitch' to buyers. Don't worry, I'll be covering all of them in the next two sections.

3 Hot Tips To Get 'The LOVE Price'

1. The best person to run your open home will be the agent you listed your home with, not their sales associate. Run a mile from agents that leave the all-too-important open homes up to their assistants to handle on their behalf.
2. It's best not to list with one of these 'McAgents' who juggles a very tight Saturday open home schedule, but if you find you have, demand better service from them. If they aren't delivering on their promise to you and don't remedy the situation, your other option is to terminate their agency agreement.
3. Your open homes should be about presenting your home to buyers in a relaxed and professional manner. Eager buyers can lose that emotional-motivation on a property if they're left hanging.

STEP 4: **PROMOTE**

Ok, so now your home is styled and beautifully presented, the next step is to promote your home to the market.

The aim is to attract the attention of as many ideal 'A-BUYERS' for your home as possible so they make that first all-important step to inspect your home.

Imagine Apple not paying any attention to promoting their latest iPhone. They wouldn't get those long queues of eager buyers dying to get their hands on them now would they?

Just look at all successful products on the market throughout the world. Don't they promote the hell out of them? Sure they do. They have to. It's because they have a lot of competition. To cut through the noise being made by their competitors, they have to promote and promote and promote and guess what? Your home is in competition with many other homes as well. You're in the same boat. You have to promote your property so it's seen by the best and most motivated buyers.

One way or another, your agent has to get the word out about your home. They have to promote it in its best light. They have to get it noticed. They have to get buyers inspecting it.

There's an art and science to marketing. In this day and age I doubt I'd find anyone who'd disagree with that statement. It stands to reason, the best marketing and promotion gets the best results. It's no different for real estate.

STEP 4: PROMOTE

You have to get the promotion of your home right if you want any chance of getting 'The LOVE Price'.

This section of the book is all about the truth of marketing property, specifically residential real estate. What works? What doesn't? I will equip you with more than enough information so that you can make your own mind up when your agent starts talking about ways to best promote your property.

CHAPTER 17

HOW PROPERTY SELLERS PAY DEARLY FOR SO-CALLED 'FREE' ADVERTISING

It's so tempting isn't it? The idea that a real estate agency will cover the cost of your advertising and marketing expenses sounds great. However, there are a few key things to carefully consider before you jump into bed with an agent touting 'FREE' advertising.

Question - who's taking the photos of your property when the advertising is 'free'? And who writes the copy for the ads? What about the description for the internet ad? Will they be providing a hero shot that captures the WOW? What about a floor plan?

Answer – the reality is that in most agencies, when it comes to free advertising, it's usually left up to the receptionist, maybe a P.A. or the salesperson themselves to photograph and write the ad copy. Here you are undertaking the biggest transaction in your life, yet sadly that's the level of commitment to 'marketing' you get from far too many agencies.

Oh, and 'free advertising' usually means no video. That's crazy considering video is fast becoming one of THE most important ingredients in promoting your home.

CHAPTER 17

Why is video so important?

A picture paints a thousand words, but a video paints a whopping 1.8 million words, according to Dr James McQuivey of Forrester Research. Here's another reason why not having video is bad: homes listed with video get 400% more enquiries than homes listed without video (source: 2013 Google/NAR study, "The Digital House Hunt").

So do you really think the home that you've painstakingly built, renovated, maintained or decorated beautifully will be represented to buyers in its absolute very best light if the advertising is free? No, of course not. You won't get the quantity and quality of 'A-BUYERS' from your internet ad either.

If advertising, photography, video, creative writing, brochures and websites are 'free', how can they ever hope to realistically do your home justice in order to get you 'The LOVE Price'?

A more serious and sinister effect of 'free' advertising is the vested interest the agency will have in the sale of your property. Let me explain...

An agency investing their own money to sell a client's property will be motivated to recover its costs. The larger the 'free' ad campaign is, the greater the agent's motivation to get the property sold - but only so they can recoup their investment. As long as they get the property sold (after all, who cares what the price is!), the agent's investment is repaid.

Can you now see how their advice to the seller to accept an offer - almost any offer - is tainted by their vested interest?

Look at a real estate agency from a helicopter's perspective. Looking down on it, you see buyers on one hand, who are searching for the perfect property. On the other hand there are sellers, all trying to capture the attention of the buyers. In the middle is the real estate agent. The agent is the go-between.

Unlike a retailer, the agent doesn't have his own inventory to sell. You're paying your agent for services, which include imparting marketing advice and sound knowledge gained from experience 'in the trenches'; for countless hours working tirelessly on your behalf; meeting prospects in person, on the phone and via e-mail; showing them through your property; negotiating on your behalf; ensuring paperwork is complete, accurate and up-to-date; providing comprehensive verbal and written activity reports; promoting your property aggressively and much, much more.

Real estate agents are firmly in the service industry. As you can see, today's professional real estate agent isn't a media outlet or a production company. They're not photographers. They're not copy writers. They're not videographers. They're not graphic artists.

They're specialists in coordinating the marketing, selling and negotiation of real estate. They offer advice on how to promote your home, but can't be expected to pay for the advertising (i.e. do it themselves). In addition to the services rendered, the agent risks his/her time and energy for a success fee otherwise known as commission.

ASK YOURSELF THESE QUESTIONS:

- Would you like to achieve the very highest price for your property? 'The LOVE Price' no less?
- Do you want several 'A-BUYERS' competing against each other to buy, or just one offer?
- Which is more important - saving yourself a few thousand dollars, or achieving a high price with the potential of selling for many thousands of dollars more?
- Do you want your agent to be concerned about recovering their advertising money – or about getting you the highest price? FOR

CHAPTER 17

EXAMPLE: If one agent had five property listings and the proper advertising for each property was, say, $5,000, that would require the agent to carry $25,000 in costs which would be a huge incentive to get your home sold at any cost so as to recover his outlays
- Do you really think that a real estate agency can honestly afford to give your property the exposure IT DESERVES at their expense?

2 Hot Tips To Get 'The LOVE Price'

1. Pay for an agent and agency based on their level of service, advice and commitment to getting you maximum results, and not on them effectively 'buying' your business by offering to place your ads at supposedly 'no charge'. The level of service you receive is far too important to your future.
2. Agents who offer so-called 'free' advertising are highly likely to be under-selling your property! (And more than likely they'll 'vendor bash' you so you sell it to the first buyer who comes along, not the best buyer.)

CHAPTER 18
FALLING FOR THOSE 'LARGE DATABASE OF BUYERS' CLAIMS

Promoting/advertising your property to a database of buyers is a sure fire way of selling it. Or is it?

I'm going to let you in on a little secret...

Every Real Estate sales coach at training workshops/seminars that I've ever attended, encouraged their students to emphasise the size of their buyer database during an appraisal or listing presentation with a prospective home seller. Why?

The reason that many trainers push this point so strongly is that they know prospective sellers are easily impressed with this type of information. It's a key factor in the seller's decision-making process when choosing an agent to list with.

Please don't fall for this.

Sometimes this (existence of a quality database) is genuine, yet in most cases it's not, or at best it's an old, out-of-date list of 'B-BUYERS'.

Most agents compile long lists of buyers in some form of database but the reality is, more often than not your best buyer will not be in their database! Often, the only way you'll uncover them is to advertise your property 'online' and 'off-line'.

Many of the so-called 'buyers' in agency databases tend to be unmotivated. They're quite happy to wait for the perfect bargain property to come along. They're best described as 'TOMORROW BUYERS' or 'C-BUYERS' (Refer back to chapter 9).

Agent's databases also tend to have investors waiting for an under-priced property to snap up. On that note, beware agents who primarily target investors. Investors aren't known for paying 'The LOVE Price'.

What you want is a pro-active, motivated buyer; a 'TODAY BUYER' or 'A-BUYER'. A buyer with enough self-motivation to go to open homes, to trawl through the newspaper's property pictorial ads, to visit your website, to receive 'just listed' email alerts from realestate.com.au of properties that match their criteria, to discuss their needs with your agent, and to cruise their preferred streets looking for new 'For Sale' signs.

Even if the agency's 'buyer database' had a red-hot buyer for your property, you need to provide this buyer even greater motivation by the threat of missing out on the property.

How can you do this?

It's accomplished by strategically marketing your property.

If a buyer knows he or she is the only one aware that your property is available to buy, then you run the risk of your buyer feeling they can negotiate a lower price. In this scenario, it's easy to see why buyers may feel they have the power. If they feel they have to compete for the property with other buyers, they'll be prepared to pay more.

Think about it.

Aren't those people who are actively seeking to buy property right now going to be researching your area and accessing the internet and scanning the newspapers/magazines to discover properties of interest to them?

Of course they are. When they find your property advertised, they'll know for sure that other buyers will be in the race to put in their offers as well, which starts the process of competition between buyers – and thus a higher price will be achieved for you.

And that's far more important than the size of an agency's database, don't you think?

Hot Tip To Get 'The LOVE Price'

- An agent can boast all they like about their huge database of so-called 'buyers'; it doesn't necessarily translate into finding someone who's prepared to pay 'The LOVE Price' for your home.

CHAPTER 19
GETTING ON YOUR HOME BUYER'S RADAR

Choose an agent who totally understands how to promote/market your property so it gets noticed by not just any buyer but your ideal 'A-BUYERS'; employing a variety of resources to ensure it's seen by the maximum number of the right people.

This is where most agents get it wrong. The old shotgun approach to marketing no longer works. Buyers are more discerning these days. They're better educated about the market. They're spoilt for choice in terms of where they can live and the types of property they can choose from.

Marketing to more discerning buyers means you have to understand buyer psychology. You need to have a clear picture of the buyers who will find your home the most attractive. It's about finding buyers who are the best fit for your home. You can't do that by trying to appeal to everyone. You have to market your home in a way that the buyers who fit your home the best can find it.

In marketing talk, that's called '**positioning**'. This is about promoting your property to the buyer who will value your home the most and as a consequence be happy to pay you more for it than other buyers would.

Buuuut....

There's good and bad 'positioning'. I saw an example of 'bad positioning' recently where an agent had advertised a vacant block of land on Hamilton Hill, one of Brisbane's most expensive suburbs, with the headline: "Entry Level Land". I guess the agent was trying to point out that the land wasn't as expensive as other vacant blocks that had sold in the area. But the problem with that in this particular suburb is, Hamilton Hill buyers don't want 'entry level' land. They want to build a beautiful, luxury home. They want the best land to build it on. The agent had inadvertently 'positioned' the land as below par. No wonder it didn't sell.

After 'positioning' your home right, comes 'frequency'.

Good old-fashioned 'word of mouth' and 'networking' are valuable tools, used by the best agents in the industry to put their sellers' properties on the real estate radar.

Whilst there are countless examples of properties that have sold using just this one method alone, you are potentially missing out on a much larger pool of cashed-up buyers if you don't engage in an holistic marketing attack incorporating all the tools at your disposal.

For example, visually appealing and inviting signage in front of your house or apartment building sings out to buyers and captures their attention. It says, "You know and love my neighbourhood, you know and love the street, you know how close I am to everything, and you know what I'm like from the outside... you've got to arrange an appointment to inspect me." Buyers who enquire about properties after they discover them from 'For Sale' signs are very strong prospects indeed.

The list of promotional resources available to the savvy real estate professional goes on and on; there's newspaper advertising, in-house property magazines, brochures, just-listed postcards, internet listings, direct mail, buyer database, telemarketing, e-newsletters, SMS Marketing, Youtube, Facebook, Twitter, Linkedin and more. They all work together.

For example, if you were to live in the neighbourhood of a property you've seen for sale and were interested in it thanks to its prominent sign -

and at some point you were to receive a postcard in the mail or an 'email property alert' promoting it, then see it advertised in the newspaper, all of those things would serve to reinforce wouldn't they? With all these reinforcements, at some point, you'd be compelled to visit the website for more information and watch the video. With every reinforcement, the compulsion to visit the open home increases.

In the advertising world this is known as **'frequency'**.

In reality it means that the more times your home is promoted, the more it can seep into the consciousness of the public – and the more chance of an early sale and getting you 'The LOVE Price'.

Could you imagine a company like Apple only advertising their latest iPhone just the one time? No, that would be crazy. Business knows 'frequency' is an essential part of a successful marketing campaign. Marketing property is no different.

Thinking your home will sell just to a local buyer is another big mistake sellers often make. Buyers these days are more nomadic than ever before. They're quite happy to look further afield to get what they want. The internet has assisted their research of properties outside their area.

Your marketing **'reach'** will determine how many additional buyers you can attract from outside your local area. You don't want to prevent anyone from finding your home do you?

So 'reach' is about getting the message out there that your home is available to as many buyers as possible. They could be local. From the other side of town. Interstate. Or even overseas. Do you care where they're from? Of course not.

Simply, the greater the 'reach' of your property marketing, the more interest from 'A-BUYERS' you'll receive.

'Positioning', 'frequency' and 'reach' are about maximising the exposure of your home to your ideal 'A-BUYERS'.

Let's bring this together.

THE 4, 40, 4, 2 RULE

In summary, the aim of 'positioning', 'frequency' and 'reach' in your marketing is to firstly get your property on the real estate radar of as many motivated 'A-BUYERS' as possible. It's then all about moving them to the open home, then to coming back for the crucial second private inspection, and finally moving them to making an offer or bidding at your auction.

It does come down to numbers in the end. The more 'A-BUYERS' moving down this path will increase competition for your property and in turn increase your chances of getting 'The LOVE Price'.

That's where my 4, 40, 4, 2 Rule comes in. Oh, and I should say these numbers are based on my experience of selling property all over the inner suburbs of Brisbane since 1994. So if your home is elsewhere, these numbers may be slightly different. You'll need to find an agent who knows the numbers in your area.

Here's how the rule works:

For a typical four week marketing campaign for an auction the minimum numbers for success would play out roughly like so...

- 4 Open Homes = 10 groups of buyers at each open = <u>40</u> buyers in total inspecting the property over a 4 week campaign period
- 10% of buyers come back for a 2nd inspection = <u>4</u> 2nd inspections
- 50% of 2nd inspections will make a bid at auction = <u>2</u> bidders

Without the combination of 'positioning', 'frequency' and 'reach' in your marketing, your property won't appear on the radar for the number of buyers you'll need. Just look what happens when we reduce the number of buyers at your open Home by half...

For example: 4 open homes getting only 5 groups at each open = 20 buyers in total inspecting the property. With 10% coming back for a second look, that equals only 2 buyers. From there 50% of these will make an offer or bid at auction and that would mean you'd only have one interested bidder. (One bidder doesn't make for a very good auction as you can imagine.)

Now look what happens when your property promotions drive twice the number of buyers to your open homes…

If you got 20 groups at each open home that would mean 80 buyers inspected your home over the 4 weeks. From that, you may get 8 buyers coming back for a second inspection. Out of those 8, applying the last step in the rule, something like 4 buyers making offers or registering to bid at your auction will have been created.

When you do get it right, you'll drive more qualified 'A-BUYERS' to your open homes. That will generate more buyers coming back for a second inspection. The more second inspections your agent books, the more emotionally-motivated 'A-BUYERS' will move to the final step of making an offer or bidding at your auction.

WARNING: 'McAgents' love to use the old advertising cliché "You can't sell a secret." This tends to be their over-simplified way of explaining the importance of advertising. Their agenda is to get sellers to accept their one-size-fits-all promotional plan without any scrutiny. Don't fall for it. As I've said, every property is different. Your promotional plan must reflect your 'BIG Why', your buyer's 'BIG Why', the marketplace you're in and your home. Getting 'The LOVE Price' is not about the quantity of promotion, it's about the quality of your property promotion. The lesson? You must scrutinise the promotional plan they're proposing and if it's a one-size-fits-all, choose another agent who offers a custom plan.

2 Hot Tips To Get 'The LOVE Price'

1. Remember the 4, 40, 4, 2 Rule. Your agent's property marketing is all about driving as many ideal 'A-BUYERS' to your open home as possible. From there the love-struck buyers amongst them will quickly move to making a buying decision.
2. Some agents are so desperate to get your listing that they don't talk about 'positioning', 'frequency' and 'reach'. They just skip these and try and 'buy' your listing with no or little marketing. If they ignore these 3 critical elements of marketing, then how will they get the number of 'A-BUYERS' to your home that you need and deserve to get 'The LOVE Price'?

CHAPTER 20
HOW TO GET BETTER RESULTS FROM YOUR ONLINE ADVERTISING

"All buyers these days look for property on realestate.com.au," our agent said.

"So you don't need to spend any money at all advertising your home; a 'standard ad' in realestate.com.au is all you need," he promised us.

"No one again at the open home, looks like we'll be waiting a bit longer for that right buyer," he mumbled.

Tragically, many sellers miss out on getting 'The LOVE Price' because they've fallen for this simplistic view of promoting property.

Don't get me wrong, online advertising is critical. You need to be promoting your home on realestate.com.au and/or the other big property portal here in Australia and that's domain.com.au. No argument there. (And for my readers in New Zealand - realestate.co.nz; and zillow.com, trulia.com and realtor.com in the USA, what I'm saying applies to you too.)

However, there are three BIG things to consider before locking in your online advertising campaign.

1. Buyers tend to be 'location-specific' when searching for property online. Unfortunately, it's how these portals are designed. Searching for property this way causes buyers to have a narrow focus. Yes, the buyers who want to live in your suburb will probably find your property on the portal they're using, provided your property is advertised there of course. But what about all of those out-of-area buyers who haven't considered your suburb? Simple, they probably won't find your property. The LOVE Price happens when your property promotion reaches as many 'A-BUYERS' (that are a good match for your home) as possible. Don't underestimate out-of-area buyers. That mistake could cost you dearly.
2. Your best buyer's favourite portal to search for property may NOT be the portal your agent advertises on. So putting all your eggs into the one online promotional basket is a huge mistake. You need to spread your promotions to reach more buyers. Ok, you're probably thinking "But we found our home on realestate.com.au." Well sure. That's not my point. What this is about is increasing the exposure of your property to buyers who'll fall in love with it and therefore increase the emotion-driven competition between buyers.
3. Not all online ads are the same. Most property portals offer opportunities to upgrade your online property ad to attract more views and enquiry. For example, at the time of writing this book, realestate.com.au offer four levels of advertising property - the 'standard ad', 'feature ad', 'highlight ad' and 'premiere ad'. They promise that the higher the level (each level up costs more money by the way), the higher your home will appear in the search results. It'll stand out with a bigger advertisement and will generate more views and enquiry about your property. Specifically, a 'feature ad' will get you 3 times the number of views of a 'standard ad'. A 'highlight ad' will get you 8 times more views. A 'premiere ad' will get you 15 times more views. (source: realestate.com.au)

CHAPTER 20

Buyers who are ready, willing and able to buy look for their next home in more than one place. The more motivated to buy, the more places they look. So emotionally-motivated buyers don't restrict their search to realestate.com.au (or any one property portal) as some agents will have you believe.

Motivated buyers will search the internet. They'll search the newspaper. They'll search the local magazine. They'll Google it. They'll drive the streets looking for signage. They'll call agents.

Let's talk about how you can get the most out of your property portal advertising...

To start with, advertise your property on more than one property portal. In Australia that means realestate.com.au and domain.com.au, but also look at promoting it on a couple of the other portals (e.g. in Queensland you could advertise on reiq.com.au). Also invest in an online ad that will maximise your home's exposure (e.g. realestate.com.au 'highlight ad' or 'premiere ad').

In addition to a more robust online approach to exposing your home to the market, consider advertising in your metro newspaper and/or your local newspaper. Take for example Brisbane's property lift-out in Saturday's Courier Mail. This newspaper has a broad reach across Brisbane, delivering a potential readership of 845,000 people (source: the Courier Mail).

Because the properties advertised in the pictorial section of the Courier Mail aren't ordered by suburb, it makes buyers look at each page thoroughly. So 'A-BUYERS' tend to scan every page from front to back hoping they'll find a property that matches their criteria. For that reason, it actually doesn't matter where your property is advertised in the lift-out. There's no benefit to being on the first page, and no disadvantage with being at the back of the lift-out. A motivated buyer will find your property wherever it's placed in the paper. However, size matters.

Obviously the bigger the pictorial ad, the easier it is to spot it. The added bonus of investing in a bigger ad has to do with the perception of value. According to News Corporation studies, buyers perceive more value in a property the bigger the ad gets. As they say in Hollywood, "Perception is everything!!"

133

The other BIG benefit of a more holistic approach to promoting your home is the 'paper-to-internet' enquiry path buyers take before coming to your open home.

Let me explain...

If you ask a motivated buyer how they found the property they're interested in buying, nine times out of ten they'll say they found it online. What they won't tell you (unless you dig a little deeper) is that they also saw it in the newspaper (if it was advertised there of course). Motivated buyers who thoroughly examine the property section of the newspaper will often find a property they like there, then they'll check it out online.

So each newspaper ad tends often to be a stepping stone in a series of enquiry-stepping-stones a buyer takes before making the decision to inspect a property.

Buyer enquiry data I collected while consulting for a national real estate group confirmed this is exactly what happens. What I found was the enquiry rate for a property promoted exclusively on realestate.com.au would significantly increase, in one such case by 400%, when advertised simultaneously in the newspaper as well.

Up until now, I've only talked about 'pro-active' A-BUYERS. But there's another class of 'A-BUYER' that's worth a mention. This other class are 're-active' or 'casual' buyers. They're not actively searching for a home to buy. But here's the thing. If the 'right' property came along, they would buy it.

Re-active buyers' shopping habits differ from 'pro-active' buyers in so far as they're less likely to take any interest in online property portals. Instead, they scan the newspaper property section. 'Re-active' buyers love keeping an eye on their local market, seeing what's for sale, what's sold, and admiring – or being amazed – at the different designs, styling and architecture. It's their dose of 'property porn' every week. When the right property appears in one of these ads, they can switch into buying mode.

CHAPTER 20

My last word on agents arguing that you only need to promote on realestate.com.au or domain.com.au etc is this...

It seems to me, many agents who are pushing this idea are those agents who are fearful of missing out on getting the listing if they ask for money to advertise your home. It's a misguided attempt to win your business by suggesting you can save money with them by just using a 'standard ad' on realestate.com.au (or another comparable portal) to promote your home.

WARNING: When your agent uploads your home on to realestate.com.au (same goes for most other property portals), they'll be required to input into the 'Mandatory Price Field' the price range which determines where your property appears in search results (in terms of price). The 'Mandatory Price Field' is part of the portal's admin area, so what gets typed into there is hidden from the public.

For properties being marketed without a price as in, say, an auction, the 'Mandatory Price Field' ensures agents don't 'under quote' your home's value. In Queensland, for properties that are advertised without a price (e.g. auction), the new agency agreement (Form 6) provides for the disclosure of the price range that will be used by the agent on the property portal's 'Mandatory Price Field' to establish the price search criteria for your home.

So here's the thing. Let's say your property has been appraised at $700,000 (worst case) to $800,000 (best case); and let's also say you're selling by auction, so no price will be advertised. However, $700,000 to $800,000 (or even $850,000 just in case it's worth more than the appraised best case price) should be typed into the 'Mandatory Price Field'. That's the price range that will determine where your property will appear in search results. It's the 'Mandatory Price Field' that actually 'positions' your property in terms of price.

Some agents will try and 'bait advertise' your home by inputting into the 'Mandatory Price Field' a price range that's below the 'realistic' appraisal price range you've agreed upon. Not only is this an offence under the Australian Consumer Law, it's just stupid.

135

THE LOVE PRICE

Using the example appraisal range of $700,000 to $800,000, an unscrupulous agent would insert, say, $650,000 to $700,000 in the 'Mandatory Price Field'. It's hard to fully comprehend the logic behind this. I can only imagine the agent does it because they don't believe the property is worth the appraisal range that was agreed upon. All this does is position your home as a sub-$700,000 property. It will also ensure buyers searching in the $700,000+ range won't see it. As I said, stupid.

7 Hot Tips To Get 'The LOVE Price'

1. Every 'A-BUYER' that falls in love with your home is going to contribute to the buzz of competition you need. The more ready, willing and able buyers you get inspecting your property will have a positive effect on the offers and bids you get.
2. Spread your promotions to reach more buyers.
3. Motivated buyers will search the internet. They'll search the newspaper. They'll search the local magazine. They'll Google it. They'll drive the streets looking for signage. They'll call agents.
4. You can increase buyer enquiry rate up by as much as 400% by advertising in the newspaper in conjunction with your online promotions.
5. Upgrade your online ad to increase buyers viewing your property online by 300% to 1,500% (source: realestate.com.au)
6. 'Re-Active' buyers tend to keep an eye on the property section of the newspaper. Use print media to capture more buyers.
7. Ensure your agent 'positions' your home within the agreed 'realistic' appraisal range using the property portal's 'Mandatory Price Field'.

CHAPTER 21
TURNING YOUR INTERNET AD INTO CLICK BAIT

If you're about to become a property seller, it's worth assessing your agent's use of the internet before signing on the dotted line.

'Pro-active' buyers make their first contact with properties for sale via the internet. Around 90% of buyers will visit websites such as realestate.com.au and domain.com.au at some point during their search for their next home.

Marketing online is different to marketing in print. Different rules apply. I see a lot of agents approaching internet marketing like they approach advertising in the newspapers. Buyer behaviour is quite different online as opposed to print media.

Here's what I mean...

The BIG problem with the internet is choice. Too much choice in fact.

When a buyer searches for property online, they're often faced with page after page of properties for sale that match several of their basic criteria.

Buyers' usual search criteria includes:
- Suburb
- Price range
- Property type (house, apartment, land etc)

- Number of bedrooms
- Number of bathrooms
- Number of car parks

When a buyer is faced with a long list of potential matches to their criteria, they tend to just 'scan' down the page only stopping if something about an individual property stands out and captures their attention.

This is good news and bad news depending on how skilled your agent is when it comes to online marketing.

So what's a buyer looking for as they scan over all the potential property matches?

HERE ARE THE 2 THINGS THAT GRAB ONLINE BUYERS' ATTENTION:

1. It's true, a picture paints a thousand words. It stands to reason then, if your agent uses a less than flattering hero shot of your home as the main image, it may cause your buyer to ignore your property altogether.
2. The headline is another quick way for the 'scanning-buyer' to rule your property in or out.

A bad headline will certainly reduce the effectiveness of your online advertising. But grabbing a buyer's attention isn't enough. You have to engage them so they stop scanning for the moment and become curious about your property. The goal is to persuade them to click on your property's 'details' button.

Getting a buyer to stop scanning and take a moment to check your property out in more detail requires some kind of enticement, a 'carrot' so to speak.

There are 3 main carrots you can use to entice your buyers to want to find out more about your property. Here they are...

The '3 Carrots' to get buyers clicking on your home...

1. On most property portals and websites, there's usually room to write a short description of the property. A buyer who's stopped scanning for a moment to rest their attention on your property will read this brief description. Here's where you can lose them. You only have a few sentences. Make sure it engages your buyer and entices them to find out more.
2. Provide a floor plan. Serious buyers will want to have a look at the layout of your property. On realestate.com.au, an icon signals to buyers there's a floor plan of your property.
3. Provide a video of your property. Again, serious buyers will want to see the video. On realestate.com.au, an icon signals to buyers there's a video of your property.

OK, so now they've clicked on the 'MORE DETAILS' button. What happens next will make or break your online advertisement.

Here's the thing about online property shoppers...

They want information. You see, they're trying to decide if your property is a reasonable match or not. Their goal is to compile a shortlist of properties to inspect. Obviously, buyers only have so much time to invest each weekend on property inspections. They don't want to waste their time attending an open home on a property that doesn't match their criteria.

Here are 4 secrets about providing the right amount of information:

SECRET #1 – I recommend your agent uses a professional copy writer and someone that specialises in 'real estate copy writing'. There's a science to writing engaging copy. You've got the buyer to the 'more details' page so it would be a shame if you lost them now due to bad copy.

SECRET #2 – Your agent needs to structure the information into 2 main sections. The first section would contain one to three paragraphs of detail. The copy should be conversational. It should be descriptive and emotive, giving the buyer a sense of the lifestyle on offer. If written well, it will connect the buyer to positive emotions and definitely NOT full of wild claims, hyperbole and clichés (like you see agents using way too often these days).

SECRET #3 – The second section of the copy should contain to-the-point benefits of the property's features (in bullet form). Use this section to make it super easy on your buyers to get a snapshot of your property.

SECRET #4 – The final aspect of this 'MORE DETAILS' section is to convert them from an online shopper to physically inspecting the property. So your agent needs to include a 'call to action' towards the end of the copy.

Avoid making buyers experience the frustration of thinking they have to make a phone call because they don't know if the property is a good match or not. Make it easy for them.

Provide enough detail so they can rule your property in. Also, the detail needs to generate excitement and curiosity. Make it interesting in other words.

Something else to consider...

In this day and age, real estate buyers use the internet to anonymously research as much as they can about their potential purchase before making any contact with an agent. So make sure that people interested in your property can remain anonymous until they choose to reveal themselves.

4 Hot Tips To Get 'The LOVE Price'

1. Online shoppers tend to 'scan' over the properties that match their 'basic property criteria'. The key is to grab their attention, then engage them with information that helps them rule the property in or out and fuels curiosity.
2. Nothing says 'read me now' better than a well-structured, compelling headline. Make sure your agent uses a professional copy writer who knows how to write a click-bait-headline. If your headline isn't working (you'll know that by the number of buyer views), get them to change it.
3. The 'Hero Shot'. This is the emotional driver behind the headline. It has to grab the buyer's attention and convince them it's worth their time to check the property out further.
4. The 'Hero Shot' needs to capture the 'magical' aspect of the home. Twilight photography really helps achieve this result.

CHAPTER 22
HOW TO DESCRIBE YOUR HOME SO BUYERS COME RUNNING

World class property photographs will make potential buyers of your property salivate at the prospect of owning it, but the accompanying words are the herbs and spices that flavour it exactly to their liking.

How often do we see newspaper and internet advertising for real estate consisting of one or two photographs, usually of the front view – followed by a short paragraph of waffle and a few bullet points of 'features' to describe it? You know the type...

"Feature packed this charming property boasts 3 bedrooms, 2 bathrooms, huge main bedroom with walk in robe and ensuite, timber floors throughout, off street parking, large private garden, modern kitchen and heaps of natural light."

Blah blah blah.

The property promoted in this way becomes just one of thousands promoted in any given week; nothing makes it a 'must-see' property any more than all the others vying for attention.

Bottom line, there is no WOW in this run-of-the-mill form of promotion.

Compare that with an attention-grabbing and engaging description of your home with all the benefits of ownership – written in such a way that you get drawn in emotionally, combined with several mouth-watering images offering a variety of rooms and angles. Done right, the WOW should pop from the screen or off the page.

Here's an example of what I'm talking about...

"Remember years ago you promised yourself you'd be in a riverside apartment by now? You wanted a house-like apartment with an enormous terrace for long lunches, outdoor living, space for a potted garden to exercise your green thumb, room for the dog too; oh, and an onsite pool for refreshing swims to wind down after a day at the office. We're happy to announce that your wait is officially over. This uncommon ground floor 'Cutters Landing' apartment by Mirvac is fitted with the most luxurious of finishes including marble, caesarstone and quality window treatments. A stunning 265m2 apartment that will sell quickly." (Actual copy used for a ground floor courtyard apartment I recently sold in New Farm for $1,300,000.)

Now some agents will argue, with a perfectly straight face, that people don't have time to read any more and will only look at 'bullet points'. In truth, only part of that's correct. The reality is that people who are only window-shopping and have no real interest in buying might only look for 'bullet points', but anyone serious about making a major purchasing decision, like that of your home, will want to get a hold of all the information so that they can make an informed decision.

Successful copy writing then, is not a matter of the number of words or whether or not to rely on just bullet points. One of the real dangers of not engaging a professional writer is that you can easily end up with copy that's either far too short on detail or it's uninspiring and boring.

A good writer will invest the time to learn all the benefits of living in your home. They'll get a solid understanding of the kind of people that are likely to be interested in it, and then write as if they were talking directly with them.

The writing style should be specific yet not dry; be as long as necessary yet never dull; be emotionally compelling, never fluffy; easy to read and not condescending.

The writer will find the 'unique selling proposition' (USP) of your property and focus on it in the 'story'. They'll create 'word pictures' that place the reader's imagination right there in your home, creating a strong desire to contact your agent to arrange an inspection.

Professional copy writing can truly be the difference between a potential buyer ignoring your listing and you selling for 'The LOVE Price'.

WARNING: Often agents claim their agency has in-house professional copy writing. Just because they say they have a copy writer doesn't guarantee their copy will help you achieve 'The LOVE Price'. Generally the best copy writers are freelancers who aren't an employee of the agency.

Here are the 3 tell-tale signs of poor copy writing...

1. **The Urgency Headline**: "Owner Transferred Overseas, Must Sell!" You can see how this type of headline puts the power in the buyer's hands.
2. **The Boring Headline**: "Grand Colonial on 800m2". This headline is as bland as they come. Take a quick scan of realestate.com.au and you'll see plenty of examples.
3. **The Copy Is Full Of Features**: "Polished timber floors, stainless steel appliances, renovated bathroom, spacious living area." Good copy writing will talk about the benefits of the features, not just the features themselves.

CHAPTER 22

Another quick check you can do is to ask the agent for the name and website details of their copywriter. Have a look at the copywriter's website and ask yourself: How well does their copy sell their own services? You would expect a professional copywriter's own website would mount a compelling argument to engage their services. If it doesn't, find an agent who uses a copywriter whose words, sell. Oh and if their copywriter doesn't have a website? Well, seriously, how could a copywriter not have a website in this day and age?!

2 Hot Tips To Get 'The LOVE Price'

1. Think back to your primary school days. Remember 'Show & Tell'. SHOW great images; TELL a compelling story. Don't rely solely on either 'Show' or 'Tell'. Use both. In other words, make it easy for your buyers and you'll sell your property SOONER and for more.
2. One of the best and least expensive investments you can make to sell your property is investing in professionally written advertising copy. Copy writing is right up there along with professional photography. It's a MUST HAVE ingredient in getting 'The LOVE Price'.

CHAPTER 23
YOUR HOME SELLING PROMOTION CHECKLIST

Here's a quick checklist on all the critical promotional elements your agent needs to put in place to get you 'The LOVE Price':

1. **Professional Photos** - remember you'll need at least one 'hero shot' that captures the WOW factor of your home (two is better). Across all price ranges, homes with professional images sell faster and for more money (source: redfin.com).
2. **Video** – 10 years ago shooting a video to sell your home would have been out of the price range of many homeowners. Today however, it's very affordable and because of the way google works, it makes your home rank highly in buyer's search methods. Depending on the scope of your home, a 30 second to 1 minute video is highly recommended. It also makes it easier for interstate or overseas buyers to make a buying decision without actually having inspected the property in person. The bottom line, video will increase buyer enquiry by 400% (source: 2013 Google/NAR study, "The Digital House Hunt").
3. **A Professionally Drafted Floor Plan** - buyers love an easy to understand floor plan, because it allows them a birds-eye view of your home and

to visualise how they can place their furniture and how they would live in it. Include it in your property brochure and online promotions of your home. Room dimensions should be shown.

4. **Professionally Written Copy** – there's a very big difference between writing about something and knowing how to write about something. A professional copy writer understands the lexicon of influence which will elevate the desirability of your home to all potential purchasers. Make sure your copywriter is skilled at writing 'story-driven' copy. This is copy that goes beyond the usual features and benefits description of a property. 'Story-driven' copy is designed to capture your buyer's attention, engage them and create an emotional connection with the property.

5. **Internet Promotions** – this includes realestate.com.au, domain.com.au and the agent's own website. Make sure your agent's site is google friendly, i.e. it ranks highly for google searches, as there's an increasing trend towards google for buyers searching for property. Check out how up to date your agent's current listings are. A top agent will refresh their headlines and copy, as well as change the hero shot after a few weeks of being on the market.

6. **Print Media Promotions** - The buzz in real estate these days is that print media is dead. Increasing numbers of agents will tell you that. (By the way, the agents saying that are the ones not using it.) They'll tell you no one's buying newspapers. Magazines are shutting down. All media is going online. Really? It's dead? I don't think so. Sure newspaper readership has declined a little, but actually not by much. For example: readership of Brisbane's Saturday Courier Mail is down only 1.34% from the previous year (Source: Roy Morgan Research). Print media done right can increase the number of buyers attending opens (based on anecdotal evidence from top agents all over Australia). Remember the '4, 40, 4, 2 Rule'? The goal of your property promotion is to drive buyers to inspect your home. Advertising in the print media increases

THE LOVE PRICE

the 'reach' of your promotion. Research by CoreLogic, formerly RP Data, proves that sales success rates also increase when a real estate agent ensures print is on the promotion schedule. In their study of 850,000 property sales over the past two years, they found that homes are sold faster and for more money when advertised in a newspaper. Here are their findings...

CITY	MEDIA	SUCCESS RATE	INCREASE IN SUCCESS	INCREASE IN PRICE
Melbourne	Online only	63%	-	-
	Online + print	**84%**	**33.3%**	**3.1%**
Sydney	Online only	79%	-	-
	Online + print	**90%**	**13.9%**	**5.1%**
Brisbane	Online only	64%	-	-
	Online + print	**72%**	**12.5%**	**5.8%**

(Source: Core Logic Australia – Media Maximiser January 2015. Based on sales of houses and units. NOTE - statistics do vary from one suburb to the next. If your agent has access to Core Logic's RPData Media Maximiser they can give you the stats for your suburb.)

7. **Signage** – a street sign is a secondary advertising medium and is used to support your selling campaign. While it won't do the 'heavy lifting' like the internet and print media, a street sign is the right medium for a quick message that generates enquiry for your property, and unlike print or internet media, it can't be turned off or put down, it's always there (for the duration of your campaign).

8. **Open Home Promotion** – your open home needs to be promoted across all advertising strategies, internet, print, letterbox invitations, etc. New open times must always go up first thing in the week for maximum airplay.
9. **Direct Mail Promotion** – today's advertising landscape is very different from yesteryear. The 'do-not-call' register and 'no-junk-mail' letterboxes require out-of-the-box thinking for marketing penetration. Direct mail, while time-consuming for your agent, is a vital strategy to promote your property to the right market.
10. **Letterbox Drop Promotion** – as mentioned above, letterbox invites to neighbours are a friendly as well as strategic way to create high visibility for your open home, particularly at the all-important first open home.
11. **Special Promotional Events** – such as an 'opening night' cocktail party might be employed by your agent to amp up the marketing strategy. Images taken on the night can then be utilised for social media promotions.
12. **Email Marketing** – upon releasing the property to the market, your agent should immediately shoot out an email to their database to drive buyers to your open home.
13. **Social Media Promotions** – make sure your agent has a strong social presence to promote the property to their network.
14. **Mobile Phone Text Messaging Promotion** – text messages are particularly useful to once again drive buyers to your open home. Make sure your agent has the software in place for this crucial strategy.

3 Hot Tips To Get 'The LOVE Price'

1. Make sure your promotions cover the three main aspects of marketing property, being: 'positioning', 'frequency' and 'reach' (refer back to the chapter titled "Getting On The Home Buyers' Radar")
2. Ask your agent for a schedule of promotions - the key here is that your promotions coincide with and drive buyers to your open homes
3. Look at your promotional costs as an investment. It's all about the return you get. There is no right amount you should invest. Every property, area and seller is different so make sure your agent is prescribing the best promotional solution that matches your particular needs and home selling plan. Be warned though, if an agent says something like, "Rule of thumb, you should invest 1% of your property's value," seek a second opinion from an agent who offers a custom approach.

STEP 5: **PITCH**

Now that the promotion of your home has started, what's next?

In this section of the book I'll be discussing the 'pitch'. It's the final step where we turn general buyer enquiry into leads and those leads into offers and bids. From there it's all about negotiating 'The LOVE Price' with your buyer.

Let's start with an explanation of what the 'pitch' actually is.

Well firstly, let's erase the old traditional meaning of 'pitch'. The old sales pitch was about throwing a heap of 'features' and 'benefits' at potential buyers hoping the 'right buyer' would somehow be soooooo impressed they beg you to sell them your home.

Maybe that worked well back in the 1980's and 1990's but we've come a long way since then. For starters, buyers are better informed about property than ever before. We have the internet to thank for that. Although your agent may still have to talk a little about features and benefits it's NOT what's going to move your buyer to the point of making an offer or bid.

So pitch isn't about throwing information at buyers. Instead, pitch is about a 'collaborative conversation' between buyer and agent to begin with, progressing on to a 'collaborative conversation' between buyer, agent and seller.

The old way of selling was forceful. Full of 'canned dialog' and 'trial closes'. Often like a one-way-conversation where the salesperson used forceful-persuasion to make the sale. The old way also included a fair amount of good old bullshit and hyperbole I might add (some agents still persist with this). While it is true that good agents are fine at 'closing' the sale (i.e. asking for the business), even better agents have mastered the art of a synergistic pitch that has a more natural, more human, more emotive, two-way-conversation feel about it.

If I was to sum up what 'pitch' will do for the sale of your home in a single sentence it would be this:

Pitch builds emotional-momentum and an urgency towards a buying decision to pay 'The LOVE Price' for your home.

Oh and just to be clear. This section isn't about teaching you how to become a salesperson. But what it will show you is, (1) Why the 'pitch' of most agents won't get you 'The LOVE Price' and (2) The steps an agent should take to pitch your home to buyers so that you get 'The LOVE Price' for your home.

CHAPTER 24
GETTING BUYERS TO MAKE A BUYING DECISION, SOONER!!

Agents can't 'get' buyers to do anything they don't want to do.

Oh sure, we could use hypnosis on them. I've heard of a real estate sales trainer in Australia once promising to teach agents how to do that. But seriously, hypnosis? That's hilarious. What are we going to do? Use our Jedi powers, wave our hand in front of their face and say "You will buy this property." "Yes, I will buy this property," the buyer would repeat in parrot-like fashion. Haha.

So let's agree, Jedi hypnotic sales tricks don't work on buyers. You can't force people to buy your home if they don't want it. I've always said selling real estate is less about "selling property to buyers" and more about "helping buyers make a buying decision."

What does that mean "helping buyers make a buying decision"?

It's about making a sales 'pitch' to a buyer. A pitch that first of all gets them to see your home as a great fit for them. Second, a pitch that initiates an open and frank conversation about their situation, their needs and desires, their 'BIG Why' in other words. Third, a pitch that helps to remove any roadblocks that may be in the way of them making a buying decision.

Finally, a pitch that entices them to join you at the negotiation table, sooner.

But often agents are so desperate to make a sale that they try and force sales to happen before they're ready to happen. That kind of pitch is what you call a 'hard sell'. Today's educated buyer can't be forced or manipulated into buying something they don't want or paying a price above what they're comfortable paying. This forceful approach to making sales happen is a poor reflection of the level of salesmanship that exists in real estate agents today.

Agents aren't entirely to blame for this poor state of salesmanship. Many agencies train their agents in-house these days. So agents are just following what they've been told to do.

Remember, agencies with growth aspirations want their agents to adhere to a replicable 'process'. Sometimes that process includes a bit of hard sell, such as, 'vendor bashing' or 'conditioning'.

A forceful, 'hard sell' pitch will actually prevent your buyer's own emotional-momentum moving them towards the negotiation finish line. The big difference between a 'soft sell' and a 'hard sell' pitch is, the 'hard sell' pitch is about trying to push the buyer across the finish line. When you push a buyer, you know what they do? They push back. So here's the thing, a motivated 'A-BUYER' will get to 'The LOVE Price' on their own steam if you allow them to.

The way to do that is to clear a path for them. Make it easy for them to go to the next step. The key is to pace yourself with them and allow their emotional-momentum to grow and to carry them closer and closer to making that buying decision.

So getting 'The LOVE Price' is about 'soft sell' and it's about removing objections before they even become objections. Plus, and this is the BIG one. It's about helping them to connect to their 'BIG Why' and allow their 'BIG Why' to fuel their emotional-momentum so they can make a favourable buying decision.

Of course, it's also about mutual respect, and developing rapport and trust so they feel safe opening up more and more. Trust is huge. The buyer will need to trust the agent so that they can have those all-important 'critical-conversations' about the property and making an offer or bid at an auction; and yes, your agent needs to be able to 'close' (i.e. ask for an offer).

Remember my story about Bill and how he wanted to buy through me and not the listing agent? (I wrote about Bill in the Introduction.) Bill's first offer was $1,025,000. He eventually paid $1,425,000 for the property. What I didn't tell you was, I had sold Bill's previous home, a sub-penthouse in Toowong for $1,250,000 six months earlier. The buyer of Bill's apartment definitely paid 'The LOVE Price'. So Bill's only experience with me was that I got him 'The LOVE Price'. Now that the shoe was on the other foot, why would he want me to help him considering he knows that he won't get the property cheaply through me? I believe it's because Bill trusted me. He knew the 'critical-conversations' we will have together would be handled by me in a way that would only help him get what he wanted. What did he want? He wanted that villa!!

For these 'critical-conversations' to happen, your agent will need to be:
- Skilled at listening
- Skilled at asking the right questions
- Skilled at pre-empting objections and defusing them before they even become objections
- Skilled at shutting up and letting the buyer talk (that's a hard one for the 'BIG ego' agents and the less experienced agents out there)
- Skilled at not only uncovering your buyer's 'BIG Why' but also helping them to keep it top of mind throughout the critical-conversations
- Skilled at closing when the time is right

THE LOVE PRICE

If you're a property buyer reading this book right now, you may be thinking you've stumbled upon the enemy's (the seller that is) secret game plan to get you to pay more. In many ways that's quite true.

However, buyers please listen up. You'll only buy a property that you want and you'll only ever pay an amount that you feel happy to pay.

If anything, my advice here is to help you get what you want too. To help you get your 'dream home' that you'll love, and enjoy for years to come. What price do you put on the happiness of you and your family?

The way I see it, as an agent I'm not really selling property. I'm selling happiness. True authentic happiness. I guess that's why I love what I do. So please buyers, don't get all concerned about sellers seeking 'The LOVE Price'. Every buyer who's paid my selling clients 'The LOVE Price' have NOT for a second regretted their decision. Why would they? They got a home they love. They're happy. That's priceless wouldn't you say?

WARNING: Agents who struggle to get 'The LOVE Price' tend to run with the old, misguided industry adage "Buyers are liars." Sadly, it's a pretty common gripe agents make. The way I see it is, to define buyers as "liars" says more about an agent's lack of understanding of the buyer he's dealing with than it does about the buyer. How can an agent have those 'critical-conversations' with a buyer if there's no trust?

One time an agent, (let's call him Bob), asked my advice about a negotiation of his that had gone off the tracks. He told me that it had got to the point that the buyer's argument for why he couldn't go up in price any further was so compelling that it had stalled the negotiations. Apparently the buyer was saying he'd have to sell his brand new double door fridge along with other furniture to raise the extra $10,000 the seller wanted. The agent also told me he tried to get the seller to come down in their expectations and accept his buyer's offer. Suffice to say, the negotiations fell over.

A few weeks later I met the same buyer at one of my open homes. It was a property that was $100,000 more expensive than the one he'd just tried to purchase. The buyer fell instantly in love with this property and moved pretty quickly to make an offer. A final price was agreed upon by both parties and the property was sold. But how's that possible? Just a few weeks earlier this buyer couldn't even find $10,000 to buy a property that was $100,000 cheaper than the one he'd just bought!

On hearing of my success, Bob was somewhat annoyed. He said, "Typical lying buyer." But Bob totally misread the situation. Bob's buyer who became my buyer, wasn't a liar at all. He just wasn't emotionally-motivated about Bob's property listing. When a buyer becomes emotionally-motivated for a property they'll often find the money to buy it.

4 Hot Tips To Get 'The LOVE Price'

1. The 'pitch' to the buyer is one of the most critical elements in getting 'The LOVE Price'. Your agent's pitch is about moving your buyer/s to the negotiation table, sooner.
2. Helping buyers make a buying decision is about 'soft sell' not 'hard sell'.
3. An agent who's good at having 'critical-conversations' with buyers is your best bet when it comes to getting 'The LOVE Price' for your home.
4. Look for key attributes of 'listening', 'asking great questions' and 'dealing with objections' in your agent.

CHAPTER 25

THE OPEN HOME SALES PITCH - DO'S & DON'TS

The moment the 'open home' a-frame sign is placed out the front of your property, the sales pitch begins.

Let me explain.

The 'pitch' is about moving your buyers along a series of steps to help them to move to the ultimate step - making a buying decision.

Each step builds on the last. It's got to be natural. Relaxed to begin with. As the buyer's emotional-momentum towards making a buying decision grows, there comes a point where the agent must increase the tension with the feeling of urgency.

Your open home pitch then is all about striving to create an emotional reaction with your buyers. Each step they make is about amping up the emotion to move them closer to making a buying decision.

This is where many agents get it all wrong. They're so desperate or excited or both to make a sale that they rush things. They try to force the sale. When you push a buyer too soon, they run away.

Think about it this way.

CHAPTER 25

When I was a little boy I used to love trying to catch the little sparrows that would fly into our backyard. I started out using an upturned timber crate propped up with a stick. I placed pieces of bread under the crate, attached a length of string to the stick and hid around the corner. The sparrows would land but they would stay well clear of my little trap.

After many attempts without capturing a single sparrow, I realised I needed to move the sparrows somehow towards the trap and then draw them into the trap itself. The solution was pretty obvious. Make a trail of breadcrumbs that would lead them to the trap.

I tried this and it worked, well kind of. The sparrows would follow the trail alright. They'd even put their head under the trap. But, that's where it seemed to be failing. I'd pull the string and the sparrow was just way too quick and yep, no sparrow.

Success finally happened when I became patient. I'd allow the sparrow to feel at home under the crate. I'd allow it to feed on the bread. The more it fed, the more comfortable it became; and then, WHAM!! I caught my first one.

Your open home should work a bit like my little sparrow trap. That means you have to be patient. You have to make your buyers feel comfortable. Let them enjoy the time they have in your home. The more comfortable they become, the closer you are to moving them to the next step.

Again I'll remind you of the '4, 40, 4, 2 Rule'. The aim is to create at least two buyers competing over your property. This applies to private treaty or auction. It means multiple-offers and competitive bidding. (In the case of 'private treaty', where there are two or more buyers submitting offers at the same time, that's known as a multiple-offer situation. It's like a private auction; and yes, if you choose the 'private treaty' method, you want that.)

To achieve at least two 'A-BUYERS' competing to buy your property will require at least four buyers having inspected your property for a second time. So the goal of your open home is to generate as many buyer leads as possible that can be 'followed-up' and moved to the next step of a second inspection.

Just to be clear, I'll say it again, because this is crucial. The purpose of your open home isn't to sell it, it's to create the opportunity to pitch for second inspections. That's the real goal of your open home.

So what needs to happen at the open home to get buyers wanting to come back for a second inspection?

To answer that, we need to understand why they're at the open home in the first place (we're just talking about the motivated 'A-BUYERS' now). These buyers are at your open home because they've seen it advertised somewhere and from what they saw in the ad, they perceive the property, to some degree, meets with their basic buying criteria.

So for the most motivated buyers at your open home, it's likely they're there to 'rule in' or 'rule out' your property as a possible match. That's fine. That's **step 1**. But what we want to do is help the ones that have 'ruled it in' to develop a sense of ownership of the property. In other words, we want them to start imagining themselves living in the property. That's **step 2**. It's a bit like my sparrow trap. Metaphorically speaking, we want them to feed on the bread so they get comfortable.

That's the real trick. That's how you switch on emotional-momentum. It starts when their imagination kicks in.

Remember I spoke earlier about 'The Endowment Effect'? That's where people place greater value on the things they're attached to (or have ownership over).

Your open home is about developing that first step in ownership. The second inspection is where you actually ramp up their emotion by getting them to imagine what it would be like to live in your home. The second inspection is where 'The Endowment Effect' really kicks in.

Here are some DO's and DON'TS that will ensure your open homes generate enough second inspections...

OPEN HOME DO'S

- Get the presentation of your home right before showing it to any buyers (See the chapter on "7 Presentation Mistakes Agents Make At Open Homes")
- Make sure your agent has promoted your open home for maximum attendance (See the chapter titled "Your Home Selling Promotion Check List")
- Make sure the agent who listed your property is actually the one attending your open homes - your agent's sales associates will never do as good a job as they will
- Your agent should make it easy for your buyers with directional signage - the agent should ensure the front door is wide open with a 'welcome' sign that invites visitors to come inside
- Your agent should make it easy for buyers to understand what they're buying - we need them to have full comprehension of the opportunity - so brochures need to cover all aspects of the property and must include great photography and an easy-to-read floor-plan
- Let 'The Endowment Effect' spark feelings in your buyer of ownership of your home - your agent should do that by allowing them to inspect your home without any 'hard sell'
- Your agent needs to get out of their way - you don't want your agent hovering all over your buyers or looking too eager - and that goes for you too, sellers should never be at the open home or around during 2nd inspections
- Your agent should collect everyone's names and mobile numbers - no contact details equals no second inspections
- Your agent must portray a positive expectancy that the seller is committed to the sale and that the property will be sold
- Your agent needs to create hope - buyers need to have a sense of hope that they could be the successful bidder for the property

- Your agent needs to create a buzz - the more buyers at your open home inspecting your property the greater the buzz - your agent should keep the open home to 30 minutes and one open home per week on a Saturday between the hours of 10.00am and 3.00pm
- Your agent should avoid doing one-on-one private inspections with buyers prior to the first scheduled open home. The reason being, we want to drive as many buyers to that first open home as possible. It's all about making sure the first open home is buzzing with buyers. Also, if a buyer is that eager to see a property before the first open that suggests they're reasonably motivated and if that's the case, them seeing other buyers at the open will help accelerate their buying decision

OPEN HOME DON'TS

- Poorly presented properties will only appeal to the rational buyer whose most pressing need is to stay within their budget - we want emotionally-motivated buyers and it's a lot easier to fall in love with a beautifully presented home than a poorly presented one
- Poor open home signage that makes it hard for your buyers to know if your home is open for inspection or not - this applies especially to apartments, ensure the agent places a 'buzz card' at your apartment building's main door that provides details on how to get to the apartment - this is where your agent's PA can help, as an alternative to a buzz card, they can be stationed at the front door to direct visitors
- Agents arriving late for the open home or leaving early - a symptom of an agent who takes on too many listings (i.e. a 'McAgent')
- Your agent is overloaded - ask your agent how many open homes they normally do on a Saturday and if they're juggling five or more open homes, consider an agent who caps opens at four

- Poor information in your brochure or the agent who is handling the open home doesn't know your home well enough
- A pushy agent using all the 'sales' tactics to force a sale - includes those agents who speak bullshit and hyperbole, run from this kind of agent
- Sellers that attend their own open home - this is one of the quickest ways to kill an open home - leaving pets at home is another don't

Hot Tip To Get 'The LOVE Price'

- The primary aim of your open home is to generate buyer leads and to move motivated 'A-BUYERS' to a second inspection.

CHAPTER 26
AFTER THE OPEN HOME – BUYER FOLLOW-UP

It shouldn't surprise you, following up buyers after each open home is without doubt one of THE most critical steps your agent will take on your behalf in getting 'The LOVE Price' for your home.

As I explained in the previous chapter, the goal of your open home is to generate as many 'A-BUYER' leads as possible in the shortest period of time (don't forget it's a race against the days-on-market clock to avoid that STIGMA). Buyer follow-up is about moving those leads to a second inspection of your home, fast.

For that reason, ideally your agent should be calling all buyers who inspected your home on the same day of the open home (usually a Saturday). The aim of the 'after-open-home' follow-up calls are threefold…

1. To gauge the level of interest in your home
2. To arrange a second inspection for interested buyers
3. To seek genuine feedback in the form of an offer

BUYER FEEDBACK

On the subject of feedback, many agents still undertake the dubious practice of 'conditioning' their sellers with 'low-ball' offers or just really negative feedback in relation to price.

(Now for agents reading this book, many of you will be a little annoyed about what I just said. Seller conditioning is a touchy subject. Look I'm sorry, take it easy, I'm not suggesting all agents are unethical when it comes to feedback. Giving feedback for agents is sometimes a case of you're damned if you do, and you're damned if you don't. I get that.)

Truth is, agents do have to pass negative feedback onto their sellers from time to time. However, it has to be genuine feedback. So agents need to be somewhat discerning when offering feedback to sellers. But the reality is, quite a bit of feedback agents receive from these follow-up calls isn't reliable at all.

Just because someone who inspected your home has an opinion of what it's worth, doesn't make it reliable feedback. Take for example feedback on price given by a neighbour. If they're not in the market for a home like yours, you can only regard their feedback as being tainted by their own vested interest in house prices in the neighbourhood.

Regardless of whether feedback is being given by a neighbour or some other person, your agent needs to qualify the buyer first before passing on the buyer's feedback to you.

The best test of feedback for authenticity, is an offer to purchase your property. That offer needs to be in writing. Any offer that's not in writing (that is, is not in the prescribed form depending on your state's laws) can't be considered as 100% reliable.

I think it's totally ok for an agent to pass on negative feedback provided the agent also discloses the buyer's level of qualification. Then the seller can make an informed decision about the reliability of the feedback.

But sometimes feedback comes in the form of silence. If you're not getting anyone to the open homes or buyers inspecting aren't making offers (and this is despite quality presentation, marketing and advertising), it's because at the price point your property is being positioned, it's attracting buyers with higher expectations. That is, they're expecting more for their money.

BUYER QUALIFICATION

Your agent needs to have a system for qualifying your buyers. There's no point passing on feedback or indeed booking private inspections outside open home times with buyers if they're not properly qualified. In any case, all initial buyer enquiry should be channelled through to the open home.

Sometimes, buyers insist that the agent shows them the property outside of the scheduled open home times. In this situation if the buyer can't be persuaded to wait for the open home, the smart agent would at least qualify the buyer first before agreeing to the private showing.

Too many agents don't qualify buyers. They'll drop everything when a buyer phones up and requests an inspection of a property. Those agents are obviously desperate for a sale. They rush into booking an appointment without checking where the buyer's at in terms of readiness to make a buying decision. Remember, a desperate agent is more motivated about getting 'any price' than waiting for 'The LOVE Price'.

There are some simple questions your agent can ask a buyer to qualify them. They are:
- What are you looking for? (What location and how many bedrooms, bathrooms, cars etc)
- What price range are you looking in? What's your maximum price?
- How long have you been looking?
- Have you enquired on any other property?

- Have you been to any open homes in the area? What properties did you inspect?
- Have you made an offer on any property yet? Or bid at an auction? What happened?
- If you found THE perfect property today, are you in a position to make a buying decision today? (Are they using a bank, have they got their finances sorted, that kind of thing.)

This line of questioning will help the agent decide if the buyer is qualified in terms of being a good match with your home and more importantly, that they're ready, willing and able to make a buying decision. If they're not qualified, your agent shouldn't book a private showing. Instead they should encourage them to attend the open home. As I said earlier, more buyers at your open homes, adds to the buzz. If a buyer isn't ready, willing or able to buy, there's little benefit in showing them the property on their own. However, their presence at an open home will add to the buzz.

2ND INSPECTIONS

Reasonable results would be, on average, around 10% of buyers who attend a well conducted open home will, given timely follow-up, agree to a second inspection.

The second inspection is conducted as a private one-on-one appointment. The purpose of it is to move the buyer closer to a buying decision. It's an important step in building your buyer's emotional-momentum.

Also, don't forget, the second inspection is an opportunity for 'The Endowment Effect' to kick in. This is where the buyer starts imagining their life as the owner of your home. Imagination is a powerful motivator. It causes attachment to grow. When that happens, the POWER of LOVE takes hold.

It's best that second inspections are conducted on a one-to-one basis. That'll allow your agent to be 100% focused on the one buyer at a time.

THE CLOSE

At some point the agent has to ask the buyer the question: "Would you like to own this home?"

Asked too soon, and the answer will be something like, "Let me think about it."

Asked too late and well, you won't get that opportunity because your buyer will have moved on. So timing is crucial.

As I said in the introduction of this section, this part of the book isn't about teaching you the art of a sales pitch, but rather as an overview so you can better judge your agent's sales performance. I could literally write an entire book on the art of the sales pitch. Maybe something for the future.

> **2 Hot Tips To Get 'The LOVE Price'**

1. Buyer follow-up is one of THE critical steps in the sale of your home. Often the biggest and busiest agent in an area has their sales assistants doing the follow-up. They might be following a script that their boss gave them, but think about it, the lead agent will always do a better job of following up buyers. Make sure the agent you list with conducts all follow-up personally.
2. Thoroughly qualifying your buyer is the key to sales success and getting 'The LOVE Price'.

CHAPTER 27
WHY AN EARLY OFFER COULD BE YOUR BEST OFFER

Aren't we humans strange creatures?

We all want our homes to sell quickly because the alternative is a long, painfully drawn out process of waiting and hoping. That's because we humans crave certainty. We're not good at waiting. It makes us feel anxious. Over time it wears us down. Plus, we already know that the longer a property is on the market, the harder it is to sell. Right?

Yet, along comes Mr or Mrs Buyer with an offer early in the marketing process and what do we say?

"Wow! If a buyer is already offering me this much for my property this early on in the campaign, I think I'll be better off waiting, because logic says that surely there's a better offer just around the corner!"

Logic? I don't think so. Experience tells me that this thinking is not only common, but those who fall for it stand to lose $$$.

You see, the 'value perception' of your property doesn't magically increase during the lifetime of a marketing campaign. It almost never pans out that way. Instead, the opposite happens.

It's imperative that you understand that real estate attracts the greatest attention, and has the highest 'value perception' within the first few weeks of the marketing process. So when you receive a strong offer early on, you really should carefully consider taking it (after negotiating of course), or else run the risk of kissing 'The LOVE Price' goodbye.

It's very early on that competition to buy your property is at its peak and that's when anyone who has 'fallen in love' with your home will make a move quickly by submitting offers. You'll almost always find the most motivated buyer in the early stages because it's then that buyers are fearful of missing out on it. So, whatever you do, don't fall for what I call 'Early Offer Greed'.

Instead, make a considered judgment, taking into account the advice from your well-chosen agent on whether or not an early offer that's been negotiated to its highest conclusion is worth accepting (refer also to the original 'COMPARATIVE-MARKET-APPRAISAL' given to you at the time of signing the agency agreement and use that as a guide). That way you'll be confident you've sold for the maximum price the market is willing to pay at that time.

2 Hot Tips To Get 'The LOVE Price'

1. Real estate attracts the greatest attention, and has the highest 'value perception' within the first few weeks of the marketing process.
2. In many instances the best offer is made very early in the piece. You only get one chance to take that offer up and start negotiations – then it's gone, forever. Dismissing this advice can cost you thousands.

CHAPTER 28
NEGOTIATING 'THE LOVE PRICE' FOR YOUR HOME

It's often automatically assumed by property buyers that sellers build room into the 'list price' to negotiate.

This assumption relates especially to sellers using the 'top-down' private treaty method of sale. So using this particular method automatically undermines you getting 'The LOVE Price' right from the get go.

Along with that assumption, you have buyers thinking the 'built-in-amount' for negotiation is somewhere in the vicinity of 5-10%. This assumption of a 'built-in-amount' is just another reason why the 'top-down' private treaty method erodes the possibility of you negotiating the 'The LOVE Price' for your home.

Negotiations under these circumstances become a battle of wills between buyer and seller. It can become quite confrontational and it's why sales can fall apart even when buyer and seller are a mere few thousand dollars apart. The buyer and/or the seller can become stubborn and even fatalistic. "If we get our price, great, otherwise it wasn't meant to be," they'll rationalise.

(Ok, there will be some agents reading this that'll argue they often get the full list price for their seller. Sure. I have seen that happening.

But frankly, big deal. Getting full list price from a buyer, especially if it's their first offer, says more about the 'top-down' list price being set too low than it does about the agent's negotiation skills. It does NOT in any way prove 'The LOVE Price' was achieved.)

So for the purpose of helping you get the 'The LOVE Price' for your home, this chapter will only focus on negotiating when using either the 'auction' or 'bottom-up' private treaty methods. They're generally the best methods to achieve 'The LOVE Price' because they create a negotiation environment where the buyer's emotional-momentum drives the price up and there's no artificial ceiling to how high the price can go.

Let's start by understanding what the buyer's, seller's and agent's roles are in terms of the negotiations.

- The buyer's role in a negotiation is to buy your home as cheaply as possible
- Your role as a seller in a negotiation is to sell your home for as much as possible
- The agent's role in a negotiation is to facilitate communication between the buyer and seller. Part of that is to present to the seller an 'offer to purchase' from a buyer and then to communicate back to the buyer the seller's response in a positive way. Ultimately it's about helping to move the buyer towards making a buying decision in favour of 'The LOVE Price' - it's a game of offer/counter-offer and acceptance/refusal

I know that's pretty obvious, but I'm pointing this out upfront so that you can avoid being offended as so many sellers often are when a buyer's first offer is low. That's what buyers are meant to do right? Buy as cheaply as possible. So please don't be offended. It's part of the negotiation game. Don't shoot the messenger (the agent) either, it's their job to present to you, your buyer's offer/counter-offer.

Twenty years in real estate has taught me that it doesn't matter where the negotiations start out. (Remember my story about Bill? His first offer was

$1,025,000 and he eventually paid $1,425,000.) What matters is where they end up. If your agent knows how to fan your buyer's emotional-momentum flames, in other words, push their HOT-BUTTON, that end price will be 'The LOVE Price'.

WARNING: It can be argued, because agents get paid by commission they have a vested interest in your property selling. That can mean the negotiation advice you receive from them in terms of price can be somewhat tainted by their alleged vested interest in a sale being concluded. It's a tricky position for an agent to be in. Sure an ethical agent will act in your best interest but there's always the potential for an agent to want to expedite a sale so they can get paid. As long as your agent keeps you well informed and is transparent in terms of communicating the pros and cons of each offer and explains the options available, you can be confident to make good decisions based on the facts at hand. I've always said to my clients, it's not my property, it's not my decision, here are the facts, I'm happy with whatever you decide. I believe that's the best attitude an agent can assume. Therefore, your agent needs to be somewhat unattached to the outcome. As I said earlier, the agent's job is to provide you with opportunities to sell and make it clear what your options are. That's all.

One of the reasons commission agents go into real estate is because there is no cap to the level of income they can earn as it is determined by their performance. That being said, why not use the commission/paid-on-performance structure to help further motivate your agent to go the extra distance to get you the very highest price they can and not just any price? You can do that by structuring the commission as a sliding scale so that a lower commission is paid if an offer falls short of a pre-determined minimum price target and a higher commission on achieving 'The LOVE Price'.

However, because 'McAgents' follow a numbers-game business plan, the sliding scale commission structure may not be that big a motivator for them to go the extra distance. They're more interested in listing large numbers of properties. They build their business not so much through reputation, repeat and referral business but through the high volume of prospecting activities they conduct on a daily basis (like cold calling) for new listings.

On the other hand, agents who follow a customised service approach, are already highly motivated to get you 'The LOVE Price'. The reason being, getting 'The LOVE Price' for their clients is what drives new business to them. They nearly depend exclusively on word-of-mouth and repeat business. So they tend to spend most of their time working on getting their client's 'The LOVE Price' and less time on prospecting for new listings.

Oh, and one last point about negotiations. An agent can't (legally) give you advice on any special terms and conditions of an offer/contract. That's the job of your solicitor. Seek their professional advice when the standard terms and conditions have been varied by the buyer.

What to Do When a Buyer Makes an Offer - Negotiation Do's and Don'ts

NEGOTIATION DON'TS	NEGOTIATION DO'S
Don't lose your cool if the buyer is acting indifferent. It may just be a tactic. Best to hold the tension and apply pressure by not responding to their indifference.	Do allow your agent to convey on your behalf your absolute commitment to the sale. That way your agent will also be 100% committed as will the buyer to the negotiations. Be aware of buyers who negotiate with a high degree of indifference - to get 'The LOVE Price' requires your buyer to be emotionally-motivated and committed to buying your home.

CHAPTER 28

NEGOTIATION DON'TS | NEGOTIATION DO'S

NEGOTIATION DON'TS	NEGOTIATION DO'S
Don't use an agent who doesn't know the offer/counter-offer and acceptance/refusal game. Agents who get offended on behalf of a seller in regard to a low first offer are missing the point. Of course buyers want to buy cheaply. Better to get the negotiation started.	Do make sure your agent knows how to create a negotiation environment that moves your buyer closer to you getting 'The LOVE Price'. Your agent should make it easy for the buyer to submit their first offer even if it's low. This will build trust with your buyer. It's just a starting point. Remember, 'soft sell' trumps 'hard sell'.
Don't start negotiating with anyone until you know what's driving them. You need to get a sense of their 'BIG Why'. If your agent doesn't know, then get them to find out.	Do make sure you know who you're selling to. Your agent should be able to detail to you who the buyers are. What they love about your home. What the buyer's motivations are. The buyer's 'BIG Why' will provide valuable information about their intentions.
Don't wait too long to respond to an offer though. There's a little known law in negotiation called "The Law Of Diminishing Intent". What that law says is, over time, buying intent diminishes.	Do not rush the negotiation. Let it simmer a little. Sometimes delaying your response to an offer is a good thing. It creates tension and tension handled correctly can move a buyer in the right direction.
Don't be too quick to believe your buyer's assertions that they can't go up any higher in price. Always have your agent test their assertions. Buyers will always say they can't pay more but if they love your home and are ready, willing and able, they'll often come up in price.	Do choose an agent who has the emotional intelligence to negotiate strongly for you, regardless of your buyer's reactions. Your agent needs to be comfortable challenging your buyer's assertions, assumptions, perceptions and tactics. A great agent will always test your buyer's resolve whenever the negotiations seem to have come to a halt.

THE LOVE PRICE

NEGOTIATION DON'TS	NEGOTIATION DO'S
Don't lose your best buyer. At some stage in the negotiation, even the smallest increase you demand from the buyer may be enough to push them over the edge where they could decide to walk. So don't lose a buyer/sale if you've reached that point. Make sure your agent uses language that doesn't paint you into a corner.	Do decide in advance what you'll do if the buyer rejects your counter-offer. List your options.
Don't ever accept the first offer a buyer makes regardless of how good an offer it is, without testing to see if they can pay more. Two reasons why: (1) It's likely they will pay more. Most buyers will say "This is my best offer" but most will have more up their sleeve; (2) You don't want the buyers to feel like they've paid too much, buyer's remorse can happen when they start to think the seller was too fast in accepting their offer. If the seller accepts their first offer, they could start to wonder if they could have bought it for less. So always try and get more out of your buyer. Buyer's remorse can lead to a buyer pulling out of the purchase.	Do remember most buyers have a little more up their sleeve even if their first offer was a good offer. Their role in the negotiations is to buy as cheaply as possible. Of course they'll try and convince your agent that they have no more money to offer.

CHAPTER 28

NEGOTIATION DON'TS

Don't take it personally. You do not have to like the buyer. Your buyer is just playing their role of trying to pay as little as they can. Often a buyer will have a secret 'goal price' in mind that they're hoping to buy your home for. They'll also have their own 'maximum-reserve' price which is the most they would pay if push comes to shove. One common negotiation tactic buyers take is to 'double-down' on their first offer. That's where their offer price is an amount below their 'goal price' that's equivalent to the amount your asking price is above it. For example, let's say you're asking $1,300,000 and the buyer's secret 'goal price' is $1,200,000. It's quite likely then your buyer will do the old 'double-down' first offer of $1,100,000. It's a tactic buyers use to 'pull' the seller's price down to their 'goal price'. The trick here is to anticipate not only their 'goal-price' but also what their 'maximum-reserve' may be. It's your agent's job to get your buyer to the point where they are willing to offer their 'maximum-reserve' price.

NEGOTIATION DO'S

Do play the negotiation game. The way you do that is, you need to provide a good reason or solid argument for each 'counter-offer' you make back to your buyer. This will help your agent argue on your behalf why your counter offer is fair. You also need to be strategic with your counter-offers. Your agent needs to provide you with insight about each and every offer and counter-offer your buyer makes.

CHAPTER 29
AUCTION DAY – GIVING BACK CONTROL TO YOU

Auctions are great at removing the 'price-deterrent' (Refer back to the chapter titled: "The Price Deterrent") buuuut...

Just because the 'price-deterrent' has been removed and you now have several buyers who are showing interest in your home, that interest still may not translate into a sale. Here's why...

Come auction day, if you haven't got a clear and precise strategy to manage the bidding and negotiations in place, you may lose the best opportunity you have to get 'The LOVE Price' for your home.

Let's just back up a bit first before we talk auction strategy and have a quick chat about the overall advantages auction offers a seller as part of the 'pitch'.

The 5 Negotiation Advantages To Auction:

1. The auction day creates a competitive environment where all of the love-struck 'ready, willing and able' 'A-BUYERS' face off to battle it out for your home. This is one of the biggest advantages auctions

have over other methods. The auction concentrates buyer negotiation activity to one day. More registered bidders will equate to greater buyer confidence (i.e. social proof that others want to buy the property as well). That in turn means multiple buyers competing, which will push the price of your home up. No auction means no 'out-in-the-open' direct competition. No competition means buyers feel they can take their time deciding. When buyers feel that way, with every day that goes by that they haven't made a buying decision, their intent to own your home can diminish (refer back to the chapter titled: "Days On Market - The Lethal Stigma")

2. The seller gets to set the 'sale terms' as they want them to be. Of course, you can vary your terms given a request from a buyer. So in a way, auctions act as a pre-negotiation opportunity. It causes buyers to consider your terms in advance of the auction and if need be your agent will have a critical-conversation with them to negotiate suitable terms. Just remember though, terms usually come second in a negotiation. By discussing them first, your buyers will feel a greater degree of confidence when bidding.

3. The reserve price you set prior to the auction provides you with total control over the auction. It prevents underselling. It can also be used to stimulate heated competitive bidding between buyers once the reserve has been reached.

4. An auction's contract is generally unconditional (unless of course you've agreed to vary the conditions so as to assist a buyer/s so they can bid). That means buyers will need to have their finances in order before the auction and have conducted building and pest inspections prior to the auction.

5. There's no cooling off period to provide a safety net for bidders. This places pressure on buyers to be 100% committed to the purchase. That pressure can be a good thing because it increases the sense

of (future) ownership of your property. (Remember I spoke earlier in the book about "The Endowment Effect" which is about a buyer becoming emotionally attached to your home even before they've actually bought it.)

However, as great as these advantages are, auctions can be a double-edged sword.
- The auction 'deadline' may prevent some interested buyers from bidding. For example, that may be because they haven't been able to get their finances in order.
- The sale terms the buyer needs may not be acceptable to you (at the time of the auction).
- A reserve price that's not reached at auction may in effect become a 'price deterrent' effectively scaring off buyers.

The simple solution for all of these possible roadblocks to a successful auction is to ensure your marketing drives buyers to your open homes and down the '4, 40, 4, 2 Rule' pipeline. The bottom line, more registered bidders at your auction that are emotionally-motivated will add to the atmosphere of competitive bidding and that in turn will fuel emotional bidding.

Auction Negotiation Strategy:

Other than the negotiation do's and don'ts from the previous chapter, sellers should have a good handle on their buyer's 'feedback price' prior to the auction. (See 'feedback price' definition in the tips below.) That 'feedback price' acts as a benchmark so you can judge the merit of the bids you receive. But please don't confuse the 'feedback price' for your reserve price.

Some agents will try and get you to set your reserve at the 'feedback price'. I generally wouldn't recommend that. You're better off setting your reserve at a price that's above the feedback but within the 'likely case' to 'best case' appraisal amount (in most cases that'll be higher than the 'feedback price').

If the bidding falls short of your reserve but surpasses the 'feedback price', you can either meet-the-market and lower your reserve during the auction or you can allow the property to be passed in. If you do meet-the-market, by your auctioneer announcing that the (reduced) reserve has been reached, at that point any registered buyers sitting on the fence may be tempted to enter the bidding and that will drive the price up further (but just remember, no agent or auctioneer can guarantee that, it'll be you who bears the risk if no one else bids). Why would a fence sitter start bidding? It's the fear of loss that motivates them to start bidding. If however you don't meet-the-market (i.e. your reserve isn't reached) and it gets passed in, that's ok too, as negotiations can continue in private with the highest bidder/s.

Every auction is different and that means a one-size-fits-all strategy may only limit the result. Your auction day strategy should be customised to reflect the market on the day, your needs, what you hope for, and ultimately will be guided by the absence or presence of registered bidders. You should discuss the strategy, one that best fits you, with your agent and auctioneer prior to the auction.

What should you do if you receive an offer from a buyer before the auction?

Agents have different views on how to handle an offer prior to auction day. Some agents will recommend that you're better off not to enter into negotiations prior to an auction. Others will recommend seizing the opportunity for a quick sale. I don't believe there is one right way. So I lean towards approaching a pre-auction offer on its merits in conjunction with the level of enquiry on your home at the time.

I should warn you though, some agents purposely encourage lowball-offers leading up to an auction as a means to 'condition' their sellers into believing what the market 'feedback-price' is for their home. They may not suggest you take or even entertain the offer. Their tactic is more to do with influencing the reserve you set. It goes without saying, this is a misleading tactic.

It also needs to be said that some buyers are fearful of bidding or have had a bad experience at an auction and consequently won't register to bid. When Karen and I were in the market to buy a home in Melbourne, we tried to buy at auction but kept being out bid. It was a combination of agents 'under-quoting' and our own lack of auction experience that resulted in us being the losing bidder at several auctions. We decided the next property we found that we loved we'd try and buy it before auction. When we found our Melbourne home, I told the agent that we would not be attending the auction and that we would only be prepared to make an offer prior to auction. My point is, it's unwise to automatically assume that all 'A-BUYERS' will attend your auction. Your agent needs to present all pre-auction offers to you and then you'll need to discuss it with them in terms of what the next step is in getting 'The LOVE Price'.

Here are 5 pointers on pre-auction offers:

1. Get all offers in writing because a verbal offer is meaningless. A written offer tells you a buyer is genuine
2. If the offer contains conditions (e.g. subject to finance and subject to a building and pest inspection), for you to be able to entertain such

an offer, all conditions need to be met prior to the auction. In other words, the contract needs to be unconditional prior to auction just in case it falls over so that the auction can still proceed
3. If you do enter into a conditional contract prior to auction, ensure your agent keeps the auction marketing on track as planned. Again, if it falls over, the auction can still go ahead
4. If you receive a lowball offer, one that's come in around your 'worst case' market appraisal price, resist counter offering. Sometimes buyers make lowball offers to uncover where your reserve price is. Also don't automatically assume a lowball offer is a good indicator of your home's market value. If however, you receive two or three similar offers, that's a pattern that shouldn't be ignored
5. If you receive a good offer that's high enough for you to seriously consider, weigh up the advantages of taking it/negotiating against the risk/cost of not taking it/not negotiating. Consider the level of buyer interest in your property, consider other offers (if any others) you've received and consider the market at the time.

3 Hot Tips To Get 'The LOVE Price'

1. The 'feedback price' is generally the price of the highest offer received on your home prior to the auction. Written offers provide the most relevant feedback.
2. Set your reserve price at a level that would make you happy if you got it. But remember if there are multiple bidders, competitive bidding can often increase once the reserve has been reached. So don't set your reserve so high that it knocks out most of the bidders. You'll need multiple bidders competing beyond the reserve to really push your price up.
3. Obviously not all properties sell on the day of the auction. Don't let that turn you off the auction method. Of the properties that get passed in, many sell within one or two weeks after the auction. Ask your agent what their auction clearance rate is. Compare their clearance rate with your city's average clearance rate (you can find that out at http://apm.domain.com.au/Research/AuctionResults/). Also ask them what their auction property's DAYS ON MARKET is.

CHAPTER 30
WHEN YOUR BUYER HAS THE UPPER HAND

In the negotiation process, your objective is to control the pace and set the duration. So it's vitally important that you 'know your buyer'. For example, things you should know include:
- What's your buyer's motivation?
- Does he/she need to move quickly?
- Does he/she have enough money to pay you 'The LOVE Price'?
- Is the buyer educated about the market?
- How many properties have they inspected and how long have they been looking?

Knowing this kind of information gives you the upper hand in the negotiation because you know how far you can push to get what you want.

Unfortunately, many inexperienced agents just don't understand that knowledge of your buyer's circumstances provides more negotiation power.

Also, I think often the inexperienced agent and/or the agent who's motivated by earning commission alone, will tend to gravitate to the buyer's side during the negotiation process because it's easier that way.

These agents feel they have a better chance of earning a commission if they support the buyer's view of the price. That's commonly known as 'vendor bashing'.

Only an agent who's acting in the best interests of their seller will be able to negotiate effectively without under-selling the property.

Ask a prospective agent how they would deal with any offers below your expectations, and listen carefully to how they answer you. It'll speak volumes as to how they'll be dealing with the potential buyers of your property.

It's especially important that your agent can read buyers' intentions, use appropriate language, and have a deep understanding of the nuances that make your property not only unique, but perfect for the potential buyer.

In short, an agent who understands buyers' psychology and is able to build a natural rapport is your best ally in selling your property.

4 Hot Tips To Get 'The LOVE Price'

1. It's vitally important that you know your buyer.
2. Choose an agent who you can trust to build a natural rapport with potential buyers, so that they'll learn their motivations for buying.
3. You should feel comfortable that your agent is confident enough to use their understanding of buyers' intentions to negotiate the sale on your behalf for a premium price.
4. Even under difficult circumstances, like the sale of a vacant property, the agent who understands buyers' motivations can literally make you thousands of dollars more than an agent who doesn't, because they'll have control of the negotiating process.

A FINAL WORD

No surprise. Finding the best agent to represent you in selling your home is fraught with danger for the uninformed.

The truth is, all professions have their fair share of mediocre practitioners. As you've read, in this regard I'm saying real estate is no different.

The good news is, there are plenty of agents and agencies all over Australia and New Zealand (and the rest of the world for that matter) that provide a professional, made-to-measure service that goes beyond the sausage-machine service the typical 'McAgent' offers.

If an agent gave you this book, I'd say that speaks volumes about them. It tells you that they're aligned with the values of my 5P methodology. It tells you they're not a one-size-fits-all 'McAgent'. It tells you they'll go the extra mile for you. It tells you that they're committed to getting 'The LOVE Price' for your home.

Hopefully, armed with the 5P methodology within the pages of this book, you'll now be well-equipped to separate the good from the bad. By following a logical selection criterion and thoroughly interviewing and examining an agent's methodology and their claims, you'll find that discovering the BEST agent for you isn't as daunting as it seems.

If I was to summarise the 5Ps, I'd say it's about helping buyers and sellers to get to their 'BIG Why' sooner in an ethical, natural way, free of manipulation and I'd describe the 5Ps as being a cost-effective and 'presentation-centric', emotive methodology. Wow, ah... that's a mouthful but how else could it be described?

Ok I hear you. Yep, you're right. I do have a strong bias towards this presentation and emotive oriented approach to selling property. Not because I wrote this book, not because I created the 5Ps, not even because I'm the son of an interior decorator. Nope, I'm biased because I've experienced firsthand, time and time again how effective the 5Ps are.

So now you know the 5Ps: Plan, Price, Present, Promote and Pitch. You're ready to interview and select the best agent to sell your home.

The BIG lesson of this book is simply that we must leverage buyer's 'core-motivation'; facilitating their positive emotion to move them towards making a buying decision sooner so you can achieve a premium-sales-price, 'The LOVE Price' no less, for your home.

Thank you for taking the time to read my book. I trust that it will help you when it comes time to selling your home.

Wishing you 'The LOVE Price' for your home.

Yours sincerely,
Peter Hutton

PS: Over the page you'll find a questionnaire that will help you when choosing an agent to list your home with.

PPS: I'd love to hear from you. Please send your review, comments and feedback about this book to bookfeedback@huttonandhutton.com.au

PPPS: If you are considering which agent/s to interview before deciding who you'll list your home with, at the very least, make sure you interview the agent who gave you this book. It stands to reason that an agent recommending this book to sellers must be aligned with the values expressed herein and 'The LOVE Price' 5P methodology. Who knows, maybe they're the 'best fit' agent for you!!

21 QUESTIONS TO UNCOVER THE AGENT BEST SUITED TO GETTING YOU 'THE LOVE PRICE' FOR YOUR HOME

(Download this questionnaire at www.huttonandhutton.com.au/agent_questionnaire)

You want the agent who's going to sell your home to have experience, expertise, professionalism and a fantastic track record.

But how can you tell which agent to trust?

Over the next few pages are twenty-one pertinent questions that will help you 'interview' agents for the all-important role of marketing and selling your home.

I recommend you print off the questionnaire and have it with you when you interview the three agents you're deciding between. If an agent will not answer these questions to your satisfaction, what will they be like once they have signed you up?

When you've completed this questionnaire with your shortlist of agents, you'll be well on your way to making a sound decision on the best agent to sell your property.

Don't feel embarrassed or intimidated in any way asking these questions. An agent who is confident of their abilities will be only too happy to provide you with their answers.

Best wishes on selecting a great agent to sell your home!

AGENT QUESTIONNAIRE

HERE ARE THE "21 QUESTIONS TO UNCOVER THE AGENT BEST SUITED TO SELLING YOUR HOME"...

Real Estate Agency: _____
Agent's Name: _____
Mobile: _____
E-mail Address: _____
Street Address: _____
Suburb: _____ Postcode: _____
Agent's Website: _____
Your comments about their website: _____
_____
_____

1. How long have you been in real estate? How many properties have you sold? What's the most expensive property you've sold?

_____
_____
_____
_____

2. Have you marketed properties similar to my/our home? And what was/were the outcome/s?

_____
_____
_____
_____

THE LOVE PRICE

3. Do you recommend we 'style' our home before it goes onto the market? If so, is there a home styling specialist that you can recommend that can help me style and declutter my home before we present it to the market?

_____
_____
_____
_____

4. What websites and property portals will you be promoting my/our home on? What's the average number of (online) visits one of your listings receives?

_____
_____
_____
_____

5. Do you use professional photography? Yes/No - What do you suggest will be the best 'hero shot' of our home and why? Can you show me/us some examples of your photography? And what makes your photography better than other agents?

_____
_____
_____
_____

6. Will you be videoing our home? If so, can you show me/us some examples of your videos? And what makes your videos better than other agents?

___

7. Do you use floor plans? Yes/No - If 'no' why is that?

___

8. Who writes the 'marketing copy' for your property advertising?

___

...And are they a specialist real estate copy writer?

___

9. Do you cap the number of properties you list? If so, what's the maximum number of listings you handle at any point of time?

___

10. How many 'open homes' on average do you manage on a Saturday?

___

11. Who will be conducting the 'open homes'?

___

12. What's the average 'days-on-market' for properties your agency sells?

___

13. What's your 'list-to-sell-ratio'? Example: 100% means they sell absolutely every property they list, 50% means they only sell half of the properties they list.

___

AGENT QUESTIONNAIRE

14. What pricing method do you recommend for my/our home? Example: 'Top-Down', 'Bottom-Up' or 'No Price' (as in auction) and why do you recommend this method?

_____
_____
_____
_____

15. Are you able to supply the names and mobile numbers of three of your past clients for me to call?

_____
_____
_____
_____

16. Can you provide me/us with a copy of your auctioneer's results for the past 12 months?

_____
_____
_____
_____

THE LOVE PRICE

17. How do you deal with an offer that's below our expectations? (Listen carefully to how they answer you. It'll speak volumes as to how they'll be dealing with the potential buyers of your property.)

_____
_____
_____
_____

18. How often will we meet face-to-face to discuss progress? And how often can I expect to receive reports, updates and feedback regarding buyer activity?

_____
_____
_____
_____

19. What's the average cost of a marketing programme? Can I pay it off in two or three (credit card) payments?

_____
_____
_____
_____

AGENT QUESTIONNAIRE

20. Why should I appoint you as my selling agent? What makes you better than the others?

_____
_____
_____
_____

21. Rate their agency (circle the most appropriate - 1 being poor, 5 average, 10 excellent):
    - Agency's website: 1 2 3 4 5 6 7 8 9 10
    - Agency's overall marketing expertise: 1 2 3 4 5 6 7 8 9 10
    - Agency's sales track record: 1 2 3 4 5 6 7 8 9 10
    - Agency's value adding services (e.g. Styling): 1 2 3 4 5 6 7 8 9 10
    - Agent's professionalism: 1 2 3 4 5 6 7 8 9 10
    - Agent's level of understanding of your property: 1 2 3 4 5 6 7 8 9 10
    - Agent's level of understanding of your needs: 1 2 3 4 5 6 7 8 9 10
    - Agent's negotiation & sales ability: 1 2 3 4 5 6 7 8 9 10
    - Agent's appraisal - is it realistic?: 1 2 3 4 5 6 7 8 9 10

THE LOVE PRICE

ADDITIONAL NOTES ABOUT THE AGENT/AGENCY

ABOUT PETER HUTTON

Licensed Real Estate Agent | Speaker | Author

"I don't know how Peter Hutton got that price"

...is something home sellers and other agents have said a lot over the years.

Like the time Peter sold the townhouse in Spring Hill for $727,000 using the 'bottom-up' method while, at around the same time, an identical neighbouring townhouse (in the same complex) was sold by a 'McAgent' for only $550,000.

Peter Hutton has learnt a thing or two over his 20 year career about marketing and negotiating record prices for residential owner-occupied property. That's how he's able to get you what you want.

Master of the high-end, pressure-cooker deal, Peter is no stranger to confrontation, and his motto 'A fully-informed client is always right', has always resulted in retaining the respect, confidence (and repeat business) of his vendors.

6 THINGS TO GET TO KNOW PETER, FAST...

1. Peter has negotiated 1,000 property sales over an action-packed 20 year career. That makes Peter Hutton one of the most experienced and skilled agents you'll find in Brisbane
2. Peter has been the director of sales and marketing for an award-winning property development company. That experience has helped him become one Brisbane's best property marketers
3. Peter owned the highly successful, boutique agency Hutton Real Estate on Brunswick Street New Farm for close to 10 years, sold it and semi-retired (for a short while) to Byron Bay (Pete couldn't handle the serenity for too long! He had to come back.) He now owns and runs, in partnership with Karen Hutton, a new boutique independent agency, Hutton & Hutton.
4. Been recognised as "Australia's Best Estate Agent" in the International Property Awards (that's real estate's equivalent to the Academy Awards)
5. Authored one of Australia's most downloaded eBooks on selling real estate: "THE KEY - 21 Secrets to Selling Your Property for More" (no longer available)
6. Peter is a regular keynote speaker at real estate conferences and industry training events throughout Australia